magickal arts

magickal arts

a guide to spellweaving, love charms and moon wisdom

sally morningstar & laura j watts

LORENZ BOOKS

This edition is published by Lorenz Books
Lorenz Books is an imprint of Anness Publishing Ltd
Hermes House, 88-89 Blackfriars Road, London SE1 8HA
tel. 020 7401 2077; fax 020 7633 9499
www.lorenzbooks.com; info@anness.com

UK agent: The Manning Partnership Ltd, 6 The Old Dairy, Melcombe Road, Bath BA2 3LR; tel. 01225 478 444; fax 01225 478 440; sales@manning-partnership.co.uk

UK distributor: Grantham Book Services Ltd, Isaac Newton Way, Alma Park Industrial Estate, Grantham, Lincs NG31 9SD; tel. 01476 541080; fax 01476 541061; orders@gbs.tbs-ltd.co.uk

North American agent/distributor: National Book Network, 4501 Forbes Boulevard, Suite 200, Lanham, MD 20706; tel. 301 459 3366; fax 301 429 5746; www.nbnbooks.com

Australian agent/distributor: Pan Macmillan Australia, Level 18, St Martins Tower, 31 Market St, Sydney, NSW 2000; tel. 1300 135 113; fax 1300 135 103; customer.service@macmillan.com.au

New Zealand agent/distributor: David Bateman Ltd, 30 Tarndale Grove, Off Bush Road, Albany, Auckland; tel. (09) 415 7664; fax (09) 415 8892

A CIP catalogue record for this book is available from the British Library.

Publisher: Joanna Lorenz
Managing Editor: Judith Simons
Editor: Molly Perham
Production Controller: Lee Sargent
Design: Tania Monckton, Ian Sandom
Illustrators: Anna Koska, Lucinda Ganderton
Photography: Don Last

Previously published in three separate volumes, *Spellweaving, Love Charms* and *Moon Wisdom*

10 9 8 7 6 5 4 3 2 1

Contents

Introduction

Traditional folk magic has been practised among many different cultures. Using the influences of the moon, Spells were cast to ensure a successful hunt or a good harvest, to bring rain or to cure an illness, while Charms were used as protection against the spells, or to bring good fortune.

In recent times the magickal arts have enjoyed a revival in the West, and this book brings together spells and charms that are suited to the modern reader and that reflect our contemporary concerns. Included are spells for prosperity, improving your business, travelling and selling your house. Others are for removing conflict or an obstacle, stopping gossip, or finding a lost article, and – just as important now as in the past – there are spells for good health, healing and fertility. Spell tables will help you to develop your spellweaving skills: by referring to the lunar calendar or to planetary tables, you can begin to build a picture of the best times and phases to weave your own magic.

Finding true love and happiness has always been one of life's major concerns, and for centuries people have been making love charms and performing rituals to enhance their relationships. Many of these have been passed down over the years and still survive today: some are rituals for courting and marriage; others are part of the timeless quest for a faithful, loving partner. Practical advice on how to create love charms for different situations, and how to work with the cycle of love and its four seasons of dreams, hope, passion and fulfilment, will help to bring love into your lives.

The moon features in the mythology of all cultures. As the protector and guardian of women, she has long been associated with the female reproductive cycle, which mirrors the cycle of the moon in duration. Many ancient civilizations performed fertility rituals and celebrated the moon at annual festivals dedicated to the goddess, to seek her help and favour with conception. Since ancient times it has been recognized that the moon can influence both mind and body: lunar cycles affect our moods, sleep patterns and health, and it is well documented that the full moon has powerful effects upon our mental and emotional stability. Lunar cycles affect the natural world by creating high and low tides, and the moon's elliptical orbit affects the weather systems around the world. In learning to understand the nature of the moon's rhythms and cycles, you will discover some of her special mystical powers. Spell-weavers also observe the phases of the moon and time their spells in accordance with its cycle.

LEFT: *Candles are often called for in spellweaving, with different colours influencing various types of spells, for example bright pink and red candles are used for romance and love.*

OPPOSITE: *About every two or three years, two full moons occur in the same calendar month. This is known as a "blue moon" and is a rare but special time when the moon's powers are doubled.*

SPELLWEAVING

Spellweaving is an ancient art that threads its way back through the centuries, embracing many cultures and belief systems. Spells are traditionally woven in the open, in places of natural power and vibrant energy such as woods and forests, and by the side of lakes and rivers. By developing a special relationship with nature, you can weave your own unique natural magic.

The Nature of Spellweaving

The essence of magic, the power of nature and the universal mysteries have fascinated human beings for many thousands of years.

Archaeological finds dating back to Neanderthal man indicate that even in the very earliest cultures there was an awareness of the connection to everything that surrounds us, and of how we might influence elemental and spiritual forces. Some scholars say that the word "witch" comes from the Old English word "witan" – to know – but it is more likely to have developed from the Old English verb "wiccian" – to cast a spell. Spellweaving, a very ancient art long associated with witchcraft, has been used for both good and ill. All things can be used to harm or to heal. When a spell is cast, it is the intention and concentration of the spellweaver that gives the spell its power, for positive or negative results. The ethical spellweaver works only with good, or white, magic and takes a pledge to harm none.

High magic works positively with elemental and natural ingredients such as the planets and stars, gems and crystals, trees, plants, flowers, birds, animals and stones. What is presented here is a natural magic that has evolved over many years from the study and practice of shamanism, paganism and spirituality, and is a blending of these and other religious traditions from around the world. Spellweaving is not separate from God and spirituality, it is part of the same consciousness. If you approach spellmaking with a humble heart, you will learn how to develop a relationship with nature as you weave spells of beauty for healing, abundance, friendship, love and spiritual understanding.

A spell is very simple. It is a positive affirmation, using focused energy. Our universe has abundant energy which you can use for the good. In learning how to work positively with these you can build your own magic bridge upon which you can walk quite safely, because all

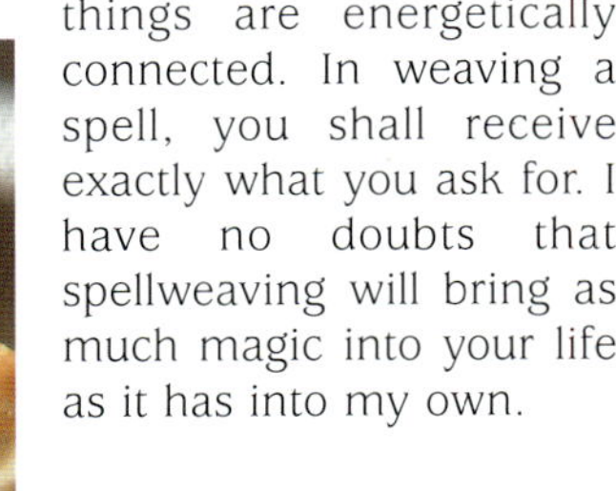

things are energetically connected. In weaving a spell, you shall receive exactly what you ask for. I have no doubts that spellweaving will bring as much magic into your life as it has into my own.

SALLY MORNINGSTAR

LEFT: *Long revered by tribal peoples around the world and traditionally used as a smudging bowl, shells are particularly associated with fertility of both mind and body.*

OPPOSITE: *High magic works positively with natural and elemental ingredients such as crystals, gems and plants.*

Successful Spellweaving

Before you begin to weave a particular spell in this book you should have put some care and thought into your preparation. An important aspect of successful spellweaving is effort; what you put in during these initial stages will set the energetic scene for the spell itself. Put concentrated positive energy into your quest for the correct ingredients. For example, if you don't add an ingredient because you cannot find it quickly enough, your spell will mirror that lack of effort and be rendered less effective. Treat your spells with love and respect at all times.

When spellweaving it is helpful to concentrate on yourself by performing ritual cleansing and by maximizing your powers of concentration. You also need to approach magic with faith, and with an open heart. Be realistic in what you ask for, riches, fame and issues of control are best left alone, otherwise you will move into the realms of low magic, which is not the nature of this book.

Where to Spellweave

Spells are traditionally cast outside, and for the kind of natural magic found in this book it will help if you can find a place of peace and beauty to work in. If you do not have access to an appropriate place, however, you can use a room in your house. If you have the space it should be a particular room or section of a room that is primarily dedicated to making magic. It is important to keep the atmosphere clean and balanced where you work. This can be done by cleansing it regularly with salt and burning purifying herbs (see the House Blessing Spell).

Your Magical Equipment

Start to build up a store of general magical ingredients and equipment. The magic weaver will always need the following basic elements: natural sea salt, a length of white cord, frankincense and other incense, candles in various colours, crystals, special stones and gems of your choice, a selection of dried herbs, essential oils, gold and silver pens, silk and cotton fabrics and a variety of threads. You will also need some paper that is as natural as possible; this might be handmade paper, parchment, or simply unbleached plain paper.

LEFT: *Spells are traditionally woven in the open, in places of natural power and vibrant energy such as woods and forests, and by the side of lakes and rivers.*

RIGHT: *Those with an open heart, who believe in magic, have an ability to see fairies and angels.*

OPPOSITE: *The equipment and materials that are needed for weaving magic are easy to find, and can be used for many kinds of spells.*

Preparation

It is important to give your spells careful thought and preparation. Your equipment should be blessed and the ingredients you use should be chosen with love and care. You must prepare yourself with cleansing and your mind must be focused and full of energy. You should also have taken the Spellweaver's Pledge that the magic you create will be for the higher good.

Energetic Breathing

The most important ingredient in a successful spell is belief. The second most important ingredient is feeling. The more concentrated positive effort you fill your spell with, the more potent it will be. If you succeed in believing, 100 per cent, that your spell will work then it will. To build up your concentrated energy, you will need to learn energetic breathing. When you have mastered the technique, use it whenever you feel the need, particularly when you are weaving a difficult spell that you need all your powers for.

1 Make sure your feet are firmly set upon the ground, shoulder-width apart, and feel their contact with the ground. With your hands resting on your stomach, take a few deep breaths, deep in your stomach, to ground yourself.

2 Place both your hands just below the sternum. Begin to breathe, not too deeply, but slowly and with concentration.

3 On each inward breath, breathe through your nose, and draw golden light into yourself. Hold the breath for a short time and feel your heart opening. On each outward breath, breathe through your mouth, as you do so let the light circulate round your body.

4 Breathe this way until you feel energized and wide awake. Then rest your hands on the heart chakra for a few moments, breathing normally.

The Power of High Magic

Before you begin sending wishes and weaving spells, be warned! What you give out in magic returns to you threefold. The energy you put into your spells increases and grows as it is released, so be careful what you wish for because you may have to live with the consequences for a long time. However, by asking with sincerity, you ask from the right place, from the heart, and this is the true power that you hold within you. It is important not to be fearful of magic, but instead to learn how to be humble and how to ask for things in the right way.

The Spellweaver's Pledge

Before starting to weave spells of high magic it is important that you pledge yourself to the light. This should be done simply and from the heart.

1 Place your hands upon your heart and ask that you be filled with the light of love. Imagine the golden light and feelings of love filling your heart and then your whole being.

2 Let the light begin to radiate out in all directions around you, so that you are surrounded in an aura of its golden rays.

3 Open your arms and raise them above your head so that your palms are facing upwards towards the heavens and say the pledge. Then bring your arms down to your sides.

The Pledge

I call upon the divine will of the universe to send a blessing upon my heart, so that I may be filled with the light of love and truth in all that I do. I pledge that from this day I will do my best to harm none with my thoughts, words or deeds. I pledge that any magic I perform will be for the highest good of all. So mote it be!

Body Cleansing - Smudging

Preparation for spellweaving is traditionally done by bathing in water. Another form of body cleansing is smudging, or cleansing through smoke. The best herb for smudging is sage, but frankincense crystals or juniper aromatherapy oil can be used as alternatives.

1 Rub dried sage into a ball in your hands and place in a heatproof bowl.

2 Light the ball of sage with matches and fan gently with a feather.

3 Using the feather, fan the smoke all around your body, including under your feet and armpits and the back of the body.

4 Pass the feather through the smoke when you have finished, to cleanse it.

Blessing and Consecrating your Equipment

All equipment that you intend to use for spellweaving should be cleansed and consecrated first. When blessed, the items can be stored carefully, ready for use. For the purposes of this blessing we will imagine a cord is being consecrated.

In a cleared space outside or on the floor, mark the four points of the compass. Moving clockwise, place an incense cone in the east, a candle in the south, a bowl of spring water in the west and a pile or bowl of salt in the north.

Light the incense. Turn to the east and say:

I cleanse, bless and consecrate this cord with the powers of air.

Then pass the cord through the smoke from the incense, while imagining a clear cool breeze passing through the cord.

Light the candle in the south, and say:

I cleanse, bless and consecrate this cord with the powers of fire.

Then pass the cord over the candle flame while imagining it being filled with warmth and light.

Turn to the west, where the bowl of water is placed, say:

I cleanse, bless and consecrate this cord with the powers of water.

Then dip the cord into the water or splash some water over it while visualizing a crystal clear waterfall cascading through it.

Turn to the north, where the salt is placed, and say:

I cleanse, bless and consecrate this cord with the powers of Earth.

ABOVE: *The flame of a candle can be used as a representation of the light and is a valuable symbol in spellweaving. Burning candles also represent the south wind – the wind of summer.*

While sprinkling the cord with a pinch of salt and imagining stability and nourishment filling it with balance and harmony, say:

MAY THIS CORD NOW BE CLEANSED AND PURIFIED FOR THE HIGHEST GOOD OF ALL.

THE SEAL OF SOLOMON

THE SIX-POINTED STAR IS A MAGICAL HEXAGRAM, IT IS ALSO THE SYMBOL OF ANAHATA – THE HEART CHAKRA. IT IS THE INTERLOCKING OF AN UPWARD-FACING (MALE) AND DOWNWARD-FACING (FEMALE) TRIANGLE WHICH REPRESENTS THE UNIFICATION OF MALE AND FEMALE ENERGY. MOTHER MOON REPRESENTS RIPENESS, RHYTHM, REFLECTION AND UNDERSTANDING. SHE PERSONIFIES THE FEMALE ASPECT. FATHER SUN REPRESENTS GROWTH, EXPANSION, AND LIFE. HE PERSONIFIES THE MALE ASPECT.

THE SILVER CHALICE

To be a weaver of high magic, you must work to better yourself and this can be done by developing the heart. To give, it is necessary to first learn how to receive in a truly open-hearted way. Use this visualization of a silver chalice to forge an open relationship between you and the Earth. This is a good exercise when you are focusing your energies for a spell but is also worth doing at other times.

1 Visualize that your heart contains a silver chalice if you are female, or a gold goblet if you are male, that is wondrous to behold. The chalice is decorated with precious stones, and apples and vines are embossed around the rim.

2 Imagine that golden light is falling down from the heavens through the top of your head and down into your chalice.

3 Allow the cup to overflow with sparkling golden light.

4 The light keeps falling from above as you let it overflow and cascade down through you to Earth, bathing her and you in golden light.

Working a Spell

After having prepared yourself, consecrated your equipment and gathered your ingredients, you are now ready to weave a spell. Each time you cast a spell you will need to create a space in which to work, whether inside or outside. This space should be a symbolic circle and must be carefully created and closed down before and after the spell.

Making a Cord Circle

1 Place the cord in an opened circle upon the ground, with the opening in the east. Step through the opening with your ingredients and place them in the centre.

You will need a 2.7 m (9 ft) length of thin white cord, about 5 mm (¼ in) thick. I always cast my opening circle beginning with the east (the direction of Spirit).

2 Close the circle behind you and seal it with a sprinkling of salt water.

Light Invocation

By the powers of Heaven and Earth, I cast this circle in the name of love, light, wisdom and truth, for the highest good.

3 Go "deosil" (clockwise) around the circle, sprinkling salt water on the cord. Visualize yourself surrounded in golden light. Hold your right arm out, follow your cord circle "deosil" with your finger and perform the light invocation. You are now ready to weave your chosen spell. Do not step out of your circle until your ceremony is completed.

Making an Offering

It is always advisable to remember your unseen helpers and to honour the spirit or energies of any equipment you use or place that you visit or work from. In making an offering to them, you are acknowledging them as important to you, this encourages their co-operation. Make an offering if you need special help, or in gratitude for a gift.

1 Make a cord circle. Take the feather in your right hand. Hold it first to your heart then out to the east.

You will need a 2.7 m (9 ft) length of thin white cord, about 5 mm (¼ in) thick, a feather, a red candle, a bowl of water and salt.

2 Say the dedication, "Hail to thee East (or other) Wind. I ask permission to work with your energies and call for your blessing upon this ceremony. I make this offering to you." Place the feather just inside your cord circle, in the east.

3 Place the candle in the south and light it, repeating the dedication, this time for the South Wind.

4 Continue with the offerings of water for the west and salt for the north, repeating the dedication each time. When you have finished, stand still for a few moments and then gather up your offerings and cord.

A Circle of Stones

You can make a magic circle using 12 stones instead of a cord. Purify and consecrate the stones by blessing them, placing a pinch of salt on each one, saying, "I bless this stone with love, light, wisdom and truth." Then sprinkle a circle of salt upon the stones, while asking for a blessing and dedication to light, to make a complete and consecrated circle around them. Touch each stone and welcome it to the circle, explain what you are going to do and ask permission to use it before you begin.

Closing a Spell

Closing a spell is done by walking or working widdershins until you end up where you started your spell. For example, if you worked your spell starting in the south, you close by beginning in the east and working back around your circle until you reach the south again.

1 Say: "I give thanks to all who have helped me and leave my request with you." Visualize the spell being taken up by a spirit of light.

2 In a widdershins direction, gather up your ingredients, blow out any candles. Say "So mote it be" to ensure everything is closed and finished.

3 Make an opening in your circle and place all your ingredients outside of it. Put all your organic ingredients on to the earth to be re-absorbed.

The "Dos" and "Don'ts" of Spellweaving

Whatever you do, try to do it with gentleness and responsibility.

Seek no revenge and send no ill will - for whatever you send will return to you.

Remember it is illegal to pick wild flowers or disturb protected species.

When using herbs and flowers always work with petals or leaves in numbers of 3, 7 or 9.

If you feel you may have performed a spell wrongly, light a white candle and some frankincense. Burn the spell in the flame of the candle, saying "This spell is undone - so be it."

Do not manipulate the free will of another, or control events to suit yourself.

Always include the words "for the highest good of all" in a spell to insure against negative influence.

Wheel of the Four Winds

When making an offering to Spirit, or to the Energies, begin by facing east and work your way clockwise "deosil" around the circle from that point. The initial casting of a protective circle in this book always begins with the east, but your spell may call for another directional orientation.The four winds are also the four directions. Each wind has a different quality that rises and falls in its influence on the wheel of the year, as it turns. At the centre is the still point of the circle of life. Use this wheel to help you place your offerings or materials in the right position.

NORTH *Time of the elder, of beings and creatures of the earth. Its time is midnight, its elementals are gnomes and its angel is the Angel Uriel.*

EAST *Time of the infant, of beings and creatures of the air. Its time is the dawn, its elementals are sylphs and its angel is the Angel Raphael.*

WEST *Time of the adult, of beings and creatures of water. Its time is sunset, its elementals are undines and its angel is the Angel Gabriel.*

SOUTH *Time of the child, of beings and creatures of fire. Its time is midday, its elementals are salamanders and its angel is the Angel Michael.*

The Timing of Spells

Timing is very important when working with natural magic. It is advisable to refer to a moon almanac or lunar calendar and to the tables of planets and days of the week in the Spell Tables, before you begin a spell. You can then plan the most suitable time carefully.

Ancient civilizations such as the Babylonians, Syrians and Egyptians had great knowledge of the planets, seasons, spiritual energies and the power of herbs and minerals. When working with magic, it tends to be the phases of the moon that are most closely observed today, because the moon has such a strong daily influence upon the rhythms of ebb and flow in our lives. Moon times are shown in most diaries, or in *Old Moore's Almanac* (*The Old Farmer's Almanac* [US]).

The timing of spells is important because everything has a point or place of greatest power. By utilizing the correct face of the moon, or the four winds, the right planets, herbs, minerals and affirmations, you can increase their efficacy. There is a right time and purpose to everything.

It is important to leave your spell alone once it is cast. Do not keep repeating it as this shows a lack of faith in its original power. Spells can take time to materialize, so be patient. Don't think that your spell has not worked: it can take time to move things to where they need to be so that both you are ready and the circumstances are right for the spell's answer to appear in your life. Spells move in mysterious ways, so try not to be cynical if the results are not what you wanted – they will be exactly what your inner self called for to meet your true needs.

If you wish to utilize the powers of the moon more precisely when casting spells, refer to the lunar calendar which will take you deeper into working with the four faces of the moon as well as the stars. To remove an obstacle, for example, the best time of the year is the autumn and early winter, whenever the moon is in Capricorn, and during a waning moon. If you wish for love, the best time would be whenever the moon is in Taurus or Libra, and during her waxing moon face.

I have found that the moon and the sun have similar significance when travelling through the astrological signs; they are complementary sides to the same coin. The difference is that the moon tends to reflect to us what we need to learn or understand about

LEFT: *The God Ra was the Ancient Egyptian representation of the energies of the sun. Ra was venerated as the giver of light and life. The ancient worship of natural forces has been very instrumental in forming the natural magical practices that still survive today.*

that sign, while the sun manifests the sign's attributes in reality. For example, with the moon in a particular sign, you may think and feel things to do with that sign's attributes, and be shown your inner world in order to grow and understand. With the sun, you may find the attributes of a certain sign appearing in your outer world and circumstances, so that you inter-relate and expand your life in a physical way. The moon is potential, the sun is actual; the moon is inward, the sun is outward. When working with lunar magic, I burn pale blue or silver candles, with the sun I use orange and gold.

LEFT: *You might want to consecrate certain pieces of equipment or ingredients in a circle of salt by the light of the moon. Such a blessing will give your ingredients a specific lunar blessing that the spell you are preparing, such as fertility for example, might benefit from.*

The Sacred Circle

To honour the spirit of nature and the cycle of the seasons, you will need to refer to the Sacred Circle of the Year, which shows the four main Celtic fire festivals. It also shows the four fixed solar points on the wheel, marked by the solstices and equinoxes. As well as these eight solar festivals there are the lunar festivals, called "esbats", which are celebrated on the first night of the full moon. Esbats are times of celebration and power.

For a lunar blessing on your magical equipment take up your equipment on the night of a full moon, and find a place outside where the moon's light shines brightly on the ground. Mark out a circle with salt, sprinkle jasmine oil – the aroma of the moon – upon the ground in the centre of the salt circle, then place your magical ingredients in the middle to ensure their protection during their time outdoors. Then, standing outside the circle, ask the moon for her blessing and psychic empowerment. Gather up your equipment, rub the salt circle away, and say thank you.

Four Phases of Mother Moon

Phase 1 Waxing
- east wind
- waxing moon (new)
- for new beginnings, conception, enlightenment
- to invoke – knowing

Phase 2 Full
- south wind
- full moon
- for increase and expansion, general fertility
- to expand – manifesting

Phase 3 Waning
- west wind
- waning moon (old)
- to release something from your life
- to let go – courage

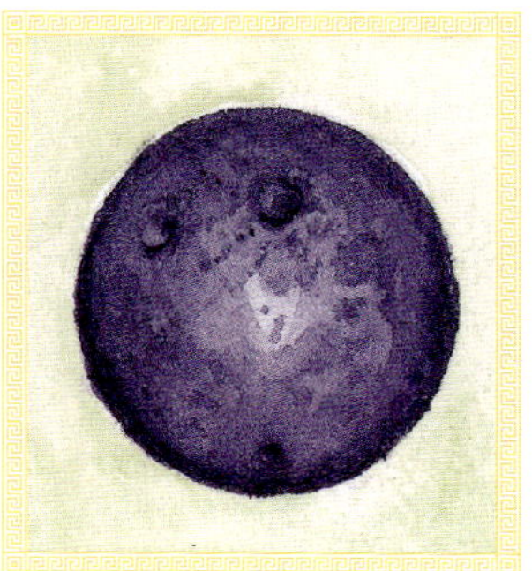

Phase 4 No Moon
- north wind
- no moon
- for wisdom, understanding, insight
- to learn – to keep silence

The Sacred Circle of the Year

Different regions of the world have different seasonal and directional patterns, but these important Celtic festivals of the year can be celebrated anywhere, following the seasons rather than these specific dates. Chart the seasons and directions that apply in your country of residence if they are different from below, but feel free to celebrate these festivals for Northern Europe, until you adapt the principles.

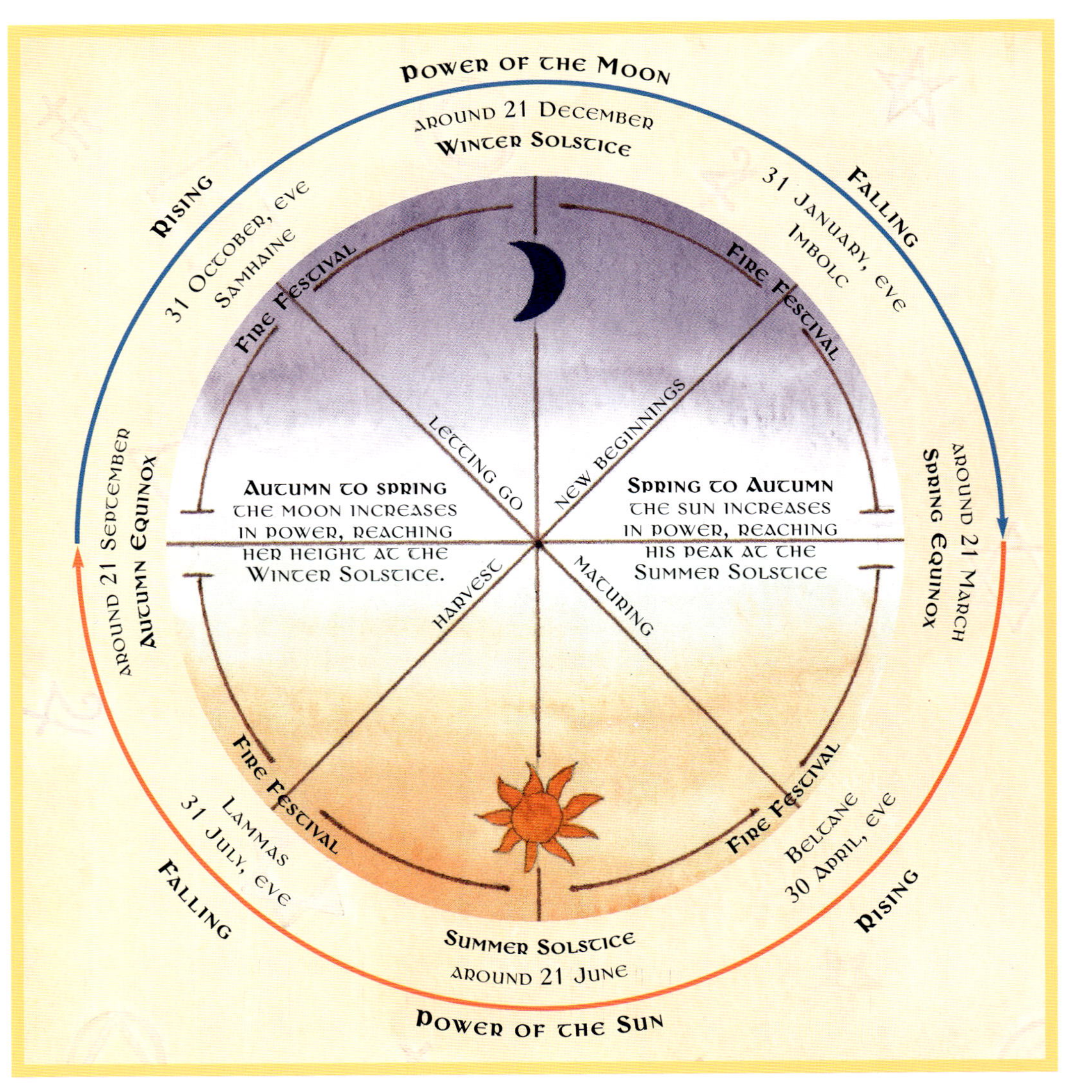

The Spells

The spells that follow are spells of beauty and power. Approach them with a humble and open heart, perform them with energy and commitment, and accept their workings with humility and understanding.

Do not attempt to harness the magic for selfish purposes, or to bring harm to others. If you do, the magic will turn and work against you. Be of good heart and you shall hold the key to real magic.

Blessed Be.

Magical Wands

A wand should represent your energy and personality as much as possible. Feel free to carve it with symbols or pictures that are important to you. Use the wand to cast a sacred circle, enhance a spell's power and call upon the energies that that wand represents. The more time and love you put into the making of your wand the more power it will have, so choose the decoration with care.

You Will Need

- 23 cm (9 in) willow stick (or a stick from another tree to suit the purpose)
- Knife
- Small, specially chosen crystal
- Sandpaper
- Copper wire
- Needle and thread
- PVA (white) glue
- Items appropriate to your wand's dedication:
  for general use add ribbons of the colours of the rainbow and top with a quartz crystal
  for love, two rose quartz crystals, dried roses, pairs of paper hearts and pink ribbons
  for fertility, seashells, river stones, sheaves (ears) of corn, green ribbons, and a pine cone
  for prosperity, coins, mint, almonds and horse chestnuts, and orange or gold ribbons
  for protection, rowan and oak , holly leaves and berries, rusty nails bound with red thread, red ribbons and flint

LEFT: *The willow is traditionally known as the wishing tree. She is also a tree of the moon. Tie a wish to her branches on the evening of a new moon if you want to acquire something, and during a waning moon if you wish to let something go from your life. Always explain what you are doing to the tree that you choose, and ask its permission and blessing first.*

Cutting Your Wand

1 Approach a willow tree with humility, and request that you can take a branch to make a magical wand. Cut it gently and say, "Thank you", leaving the small crystal as a gift.

2 While still standing with the tree and with the branch in your hand, ask for her blessing upon your magical wand by circling the tree clockwise three times, saying:

Mother willow – tree of wishes, bless this wand with light. Earth, Air, Fire and Water, bless with your magic bright.
Angels of the heavens, circle this around, spiral through this magic wand, to guide it well and right.

The Seven Sacred Trees of the Week

A wand of the right length should be both cut from its tree, and used in a spell, on the right day.

Saturday	Alder 7.5 cm (3 in)
Sunday	Birch 15 cm (6 in)
Monday	Willow 23 cm (9 in)
Tuesday	Holly 13 cm (5 in)
Wednesday	Ash 20 cm (8 in)
Thursday	Oak 10 cm (4 in)
Friday	Apple 18 cm (7 in)

Decorating Your Wand

1 Strip the bark away from the central wand and sand it down with coarse sandpaper. Sand it again with fine sandpaper until the wand is completely smooth.

2 Decorate the wand with appropriate items and ribbons. For general use, top the wand with a clear quartz crystal, binding it to the wand with copper wire, then glue bands of ribbons in the seven colours of the rainbow along its length. Use copper wire or a needle and thread to add anything else that feels right to you, such as a charm or tiny bells.

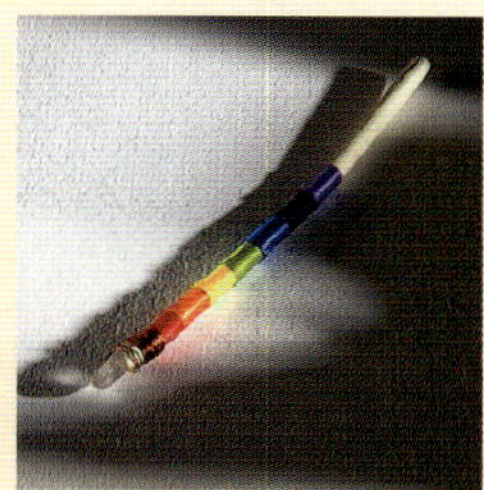

LEFT: *For a general wand, use these materials and add any personal item which you feel has particular significance or potency for you.*

LEFT: *The colour pink and roses are associated with love; use these symbols to decorate your wand for a love spell.*

LEFT: *These symbols of growth and fertility will give a fertility spell greater power. Larger items like these will need a sturdy wand. Use copper wire to attach them firmly.*

Love Spell

Ask for someone to share your love with but do not name anyone, otherwise you will be trying to control his or her free will. Whoever answers will be right for your needs.

You Will Need

- Bottle of rose water
- 2.7 m (9 ft) white cord
- 4 green candles
- Charcoal and heatproof burner
- Pink candle
- Rose petals
- Rose essential oil
- Cinnamon stick
- Gold pen
- Glass bowl, filled with spring water

Environment

This spell is to be performed on a Friday, during a waxing (new) moon.

Preparation

Cleanse yourself first by having a bath or shower then scent yourself with rose water.

1 Open your cord circle. Consecrate yourself by smudging. Instead of making different offerings to the four directions, light a green candle in each direction and invoke the winds:

Hail to thee, East/ South/ West/ North Wind. I call for love and make this offering of light to you.

2 Place some charcoal in a heatproof burner in the centre of the circle and light it. Light a pink candle next to it. Begin your energetic breathing until you feel emotionally charged.

3 You are calling for new beginnings, so face east. Put seven rose petals to one side then rub rose oil into the rest. Crush the cinnamon stick and place with the scented rose petals on the burning charcoal.

4 Focus your heart upon feeling love. Write the word "Love" in gold ink upon the seven petals you put to one side. Place them gently on the bowl of water.

ABOVE: *The dove is symbolic of Venus – planet of love and peace – and so dove feathers can be used when working a spell for love, romance or friendship.*

5 Sit in the circle breathing in the scent of rose and cinnamon. Take time to centre and build up your charged energy. Open your hands, open your heart and speak your request seven times, with as much genuine feeling and emotion as possible:

O Angel Anael, I call upon you to fill me with love, that I may feel a joyous heart. I ask that I may share this love with another who will come to me of his/her free will and together we shall know the beauty of a loving union. I ask this for the highest good of all.

6 Say "Thank you" at the end of the seventh request. Blow out the candles, close your spell and then your cord circle widdershins. Pour the rose petals and water respectfully upon the earth, or in a container of earth.

Spell to Remove an Obstacle

Your gift to Mother Earth, in return for helping you, can be something you have made yourself such as a cake or a piece of embroidery. It can also be a loving action such as picking up litter, clearing a stream or planting a tree.

You Will Need

- A gift for Mother Earth
- A fossil or blessed stone
- Natural sea salt

Environment

Choose somewhere natural, safe and outdoors, where you feel comfortable and welcome. This spell is to be performed on a Saturday, on the fourth day after the first day of a full moon.

Preparation

Carry your stone or fossil with you for seven days, from a Saturday to a Saturday. Talk to it, tell it your troubles, become its friend. Perform your spell on the seventh day, Saturday.

1 Take your gift and fossil to the place you have chosen to perform your spell. Beginning with the east, with the salt draw a deosil circle around yourself large enough to sit in, repeating the opening circle invocation.

2 Place yourself comfortably on the ground, facing north. Say the following invocation three times with as much feeling as possible:

Mother Earth, I bring you a gift of (state what it is) **because I have come to you today to ask you to help me. I wish to remove** (state your obstacle)**.**
I ask you with all my heart if you will talk with the Angel Cassiel on my behalf and both of you help me to lift the condition by helping me to understand why it is here, so that I may move forward safe in the knowledge that I am part of a loving universe. Teach me, Mother Earth, to be wise and to trust in the beauty of all life. Show me the way to remove this obstacle so that I may grow in understanding and wisdom.
(Take your fossil.)
I ask that this fossil, when it is buried in your being, may take away my burden and help me to endure, because it is within you and you are with me.

Fossils

Fossils link us to our ancestors and to earth's wisdom because of their long existence on the planet.

3 Say "Thank you" after the final round. Bury your fossil. Send the energies home by saying "So mote it be", while visualizing the completion of your task.

4 Leave the earth your gift, or tell her your pledge has been done (or will be done) on a certain date. With spellweaving it is important to give, or you may not receive.

5 Starting with the west, break your circle of salt widdershins and brush it away into the surrounding area, until you are back at west again. Walk away, leaving your troubles buried behind you. Do not look back.

RIGHT: *The earth has an inherent ability to help us transmute our negative patterns and difficulties, rather like old vegetable peelings, which under her influence become high-quality compost.*

Prosperity Spell

In order for prosperity to come to you, you need first to give something of yourself freely, trusting that you will be repaid. The blessed silver coin will mean that you get as much help as possible when you are ready to weave your spell.

You Will Need

- Blessed silver coin
- 2.7 m (9 ft) white cord
- Four large pinches of tobacco
- Gold candle
- 15 cm (6 in) square of orange silk
- Fresh spearmint leaves
- Orange thread

Environment

Choose somewhere warm and private.

This spell is to be performed on a Sunday, during a waxing (new) moon.

Preparation

Carry the coin with you for seven days, from a Sunday to a Sunday. Perform your spellweaving on the seventh day, Sunday. Within the seven days, give something of yourself that costs time and energy, such as helping another, without payment. Offer your gift to the Angel Michael. He will know that you are prepared to make an effort towards prosperity.

1 Open your circle. Begin with the east, making offerings of tobacco to each of the four directions. Stand in the centre of the four points marked with tobacco. Light your candle.

2 Take out your silver coin and hold it in the palm of your left hand. Hold the gold candle in the other hand. Repeat the invocation while facing south and passing your coin through the flame of the candle six times:

O Angel Michael, I ask you to help me to understand the nature of abundance, that I may become wealthy in spirit as well as financially. I ask you to bring me the riches that I need in order to live comfortably. I ask for the right amount of prosperity to fill my life that will meet my needs and so give me the time and energy to use my gifts, to celebrate life and to help others in poverty or unhappiness. Grant me this and I will remember to give as I have received.

3 Say "Thank you" after the sixth request. Place the coin in the orange silk square with some spearmint leaves and bind with orange thread. Carry this with you in your coin purse, or keep it in a container made of tin (the metal of Jupiter) in your home.

LEFT: *Tobacco is one of the sacred herbs of the Native Americans and is used in certain ceremonies to call in the energies. In magical terms, tobacco is sacred to Mars and is used in this spell to increase the strength and power of the wish.*

4 Moving widdershins, gather up the four pinches of tobacco, saying "Thank you" to each of the four directions as you do so. When you have all four pinches in your hand, say "So mote it be" and visualize the spell being carried into the universe.

5 Place the tobacco underneath a tree, an almond or horse chestnut if possible, or an oak or field maple.

Silver Coin

Take care of the coin, as losing it could indicate that you are forgetful or irresponsible with your money. If you do lose it, don't worry too much as it may mean that your finances will improve gradually rather than suddenly, or that money is not the answer at the moment. Replace the coin with one that you have passed through the flame of a gold candle six times. If this also gets lost, wait for 28 days before you attempt the spell again.

Travel Spell

For safe journeying, find an unusual stone and mark it with the alchemical symbol for air, which is the wind for travellers. Take it with you to ensure your own safe passage, or give it to someone else to carry until they return.

You Will Need

- An unusual stone from your area
- 2.7 m (9 ft) white cord
- Yellow candle, blessed
- Lavender incense or essential oil
- Aromatherapy burner (if necessary)
- Yellow and violet paints
- Artist's paintbrush

Environment

This spell is to be performed on a Wednesday.

Preparation

Find a stone that is different in some way from other stones in your area, perhaps in colour, shape or size. Take it home with you, asking permission of it first.

1 Open your cord circle and honour the four directions. Place the yellow candle and lavender incense or essential oil in the centre of the circle and light them.

2 Facing east, paint your stone yellow then draw a triangle in violet, with a line near its base, as shown. This is the alchemical symbol for air.

3 Hold the stone up to the east and as you do so, say the invocation eight times, making sure that you say "Thank you" after the eighth:

St Christopher is the patron saint of travellers. Medallions with his image are often given as gifts to loved ones who travel or move away.

O Raphael, Angel of the East, fill this stone with your blessing and protection. I pray to you for a safe journey for me (or someone else's name)**. Guard me** (or other) **and guide me** (or other) **on the path this journey takes, until I** (or other) **can return.**

4 Close your spell and circle in the usual way. Carry your stone with you on your journey.

Spell to Improve Your Business

Repeat this spell regularly to keep your business affairs flowing smoothly. Giving a gift to the energies that are helping you with your business pleases them and encourages them to work positively on your behalf.

You Will Need

- 3, 7 or 9 fresh basil leaves
- Bowl of spring water
- Citrine
- Dried ears of corn
- Rice grains
- Mint leaves

Environment

This spell can be performed once a month on the first day of a new moon.

1 Bless your equipment and ingredients. Soak the basil leaves in the bowl of water for about 1 hour, stirring occasionally in a deosil direction.

2 Beginning to the right of the entrance, walk deosil around your building or work area, sprinkling the aromatic water as you go and repeating the invocation:

**Business expand, business grow,
secure and successful –
my dealings flow.**

3 Rice and corn symbolize new life and will encourage fertile opportunities in your business. Bless the citrine, corn, rice and mint leaves, then place the citrine where you keep your money or transactions. Offer the corn and the rice to the energies that are helping you with your business generally, by sprinkling them in discreet places around your office or workplace.

4 Carry the mint leaves in your money pocket. Replace them with fresh ones each time you re-work the spell.

Psychic Protection Spell

These spells will safely remove any negative vibrations from your home or from yourself by burying them in the earth. Be careful not to inadvertently send out any ill will in return.

You Will Need

- Pieces of flint
- Onions (1 for each room in your house)
- Red thread
- Red fabric
- Garlic clove
- Rosemary sprigs
- Red candle
- Frankincense
- Carnelian stone
- Vervain

Environment

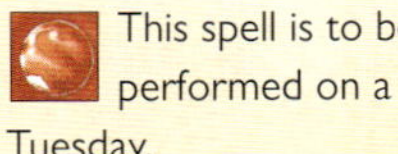

This spell is to be performed on a Tuesday.

Spell for Your Home

1 Place the pieces of flint in the centre of the area of your home you feel most uncomfortable in. Ask the flints the following:

Please become my helpers in removing any negative psychic energy from my environment. I ask that you become the focus of any negativity towards this place and thank you, Grandfather and Grandmother stones, for helping me.

2 Leave the flints alone while you continue with the next stage. Peel one onion for each room. Suspend each one on a red thread and hang them at windows in various parts of your home, repeating the following:

I ask that this onion absorb all negative vibrations that are entering this place. Thank you.

3 Leave the onions in place for seven days, then gather them up into the red fabric with a clove of garlic, making sure that you do not touch them with your bare skin. Tie the fabric with a red thread and take it outside the boundaries of your home, preferably at a crossroads. Bury it, saying:

Mother, I bring you these for your cleansing touch.

4 Collect your pieces of flint and place one either side and outside the doorways to your property. Place the others in the corners of the boundary to your garden or land, re-affirming your request that they remain the absorbers of any negative psychic activity.

5 Place rosemary sprigs on all the windowsills, then light the red candle and frankincense. As they burn, visualize your home surrounded in a globe of golden light, with blue flames around the outside. Call for:

Peace in all universes – may all who wish harm be healed of their ignorance.

6 Do not use this candle again. Once the spell is completed, bury it as you did the onions.

RIGHT: *Vervain is used in magic to protect, enhance and purify. Anointing your magical equipment with vervain will ensure that you and they are kept clean and protected.*

Protection for Yourself

Visualize yourself enclosed in a golden globe of pale blue light, with orange flames around the circumference. Repeat this powerful invocation once only:

Ring Pass Not

OR Cross your arms, legs and as many fingers and toes as you can, whenever you feel under attack. Visualize yourself in a ball of violet light. Imagine that you are inside a circular mirror, with the glass pointing outwards. Visualize that all negativity is now being reflected back to the sender. Keep your own feelings separate and send no ill will in return.

OR Carry a blessed carnelian stone anointed with vervain flower essence or a sprig of the vervain herb itself, wrapped in a piece of red cloth that is tied with red thread.

Carnelian Stone

Carnelian has the ability to protect you from negativity and helps to stabilize unbalanced energy in your surroundings. The stone is connected to hara, the personal power centre or Shaman's Cave, and so links you to your own inner power and strength during times of psychic stress.

Spell for Good Health

Each planet has its own magic square which can be used to harness its powers. The Magic Square of the Sun is used in this spell for health, it can also be used for success and prosperity.

You Will Need

- 2.7 m (9 ft) white cord
- Gold candle
- Frankincense
- Gold pen
- 15 cm (6 in) square of natural paper
- Ruler

Environment

This spell is to be performed on a Sunday during a waxing (new) or full moon.

1 Open your circle taking with you all the ingredients for the spell. Put the gold candle and frankincense in the centre and light them. Sitting facing south inside the circle, translate your first name into numbers by using the numbers below. For example, the name Mary becomes 4197.

1	2	3	4	5	6	7	8	9
A	B	C	D	E	F	G	H	I
J	K	L	M	N	O	P	Q	R
S	T	U	V	W	X	Y	Z	

2 Use the Magic Square of the Sun to work out the sigil of your name by drawing a line through the appropriate numbers so that it forms a pattern. For example, Mary – 4197 – becomes the sigil shown opposite.

6	32	3	34	35	1
7	11	27	28	8	30
19	14	16	15	23	24
18	20	22	21	17	13
25	29	10	9	26	12
36	5	33	4	2	31

The Magic Square of the Sun

Use the square to mark out the sigil of your name. The sigil for Mary has been added here. Use the Magic Square of the Sun for invocations for health, wealth and success.

LEFT: *This is the sigil of the sun. copy it onto your piece of paper to increase the power of the spell.*

3 Using the gold pen, mark a 7.5 cm (3 in) square in the top right-hand corner of the paper. Draw your sigil in this square. On the back of the piece of paper copy the sigil of the sun and the words "Angel Och".

4 Hold the piece of paper to your heart, with your sigil facing inwards, and visualize golden orange light filling your heart and then the whole of your body. Repeat:

I am healthy and well.

5 Then take a strand of your hair and lay it on the spell. Fold the piece of paper six times so that it forms a small packet. Keep it in a very safe place, or preferably carry it with you near to your heart.

Female Fertility Garland

It is very important that this spell is performed on the first day of the full moon. Weave a circle of hazel twigs to make a garland then invoke Diana, the goddess of fertility, as you decorate it with nuts and pine cones gathered in the woods or forest.

You Will Need

- 2.7 m (9 ft) white cord
- Aromatherapy burner
- Jasmine oil
- Green candle
- Hazel twigs
- Green thread
- Acorns, walnuts, hazelnuts and/or pine cones
- Cinnamon sticks
- Green ribbon
- Rice wine (optional)

Environment

This spell is to be performed on a Monday after your menstruation is completely finished, and on the first day of a full moon.

1 Bless, consecrate and open your cord circle. Place the aromatherapy burner filled with nine drops of jasmine oil in the centre, saying as you light it:

Hail to you, Levanah. I honour your presence with this aroma and ask you to help me with my request.

Light the green candle, while saying:

Hail to thee, Nogah. I honour you with this flame of light and ask you to help me with my request.

Point your right hand to the heavens and say:

Father of the skies, I ask for the fertile seed of life to enter me.

Touch the earth with your left hand and say:

Mother of the earth, I ask for the egg of life to be made fertile.

2 Sit down on the ground, facing south. Weave the hazel twigs together to make a circle and bind them with green thread.

3 Take the nuts and cones and pour out nine drops of jasmine oil. Anoint each nut or cone with oil, saying the following invocation with intense feeling:

ABOVE: *Nuts and pine cones and rice have long been associated with fertility spells. Cinnamon, a potent spice of the sun, is used to represent male energy and to increase the passion and vigour of this spell.*

O Diana, goddess of fertility. I call to you that I may carry and bear a child who shall be born of love and cherished as a child of blessed life. Grant my wish and help me to conceive.

Say this nine times, saying: “Thank you” at the ninth request. Visualize new life entering and filling you as you attach the nuts and cones to your garland.

4 Decorate the garland with cinnamon sticks and green ribbon, and sprinkle it with rice wine if you wish. When the garland is completed, stand up and say:

SO MOTE IT BE, MAY DIVINE WILL BE DONE.

5 Beginning in the east, close your spell widdershins first and then your circle. Gather all the organic ingredients and dispose of them on the earth outside.

6 Place the garland above your nuptial bed. If it is biologically possible for you to conceive it should now happen, you must just relax and let it take place in its right time. If you suspect that you have any medical problems you must consult a medical practitioner.

GINGER AND PASSION

Gently inhaling the aroma of some fresh ginger root stimulates passion and desire in the male. Females can carry a small piece of ginger root to arouse a man's passion. Men, too, can carry a piece of it to increase their sexual magnetism. Ginger tea is a good drink for lovers to drink together to increase their sexual energy.

House Blessing Spell

If you have moved into a new house, as well as performing this spell you can also sweep each room with a birch broom. Work clockwise and sweep into the centre, imagining unseen psychic matter being swept up as well. Gather the sweepings in a paper carrier bag and empty it in the garden or burn it outside.

You Will Need

- Natural sea salt
- Small bowl
- Rose geranium oil
- White candle
- Aromatherapy burner
- Spring water
- A few grains of organic rice
- 15 cm (6 in) square of golden fabric

Environment

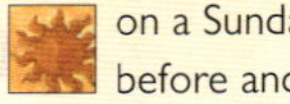

This spell should only be performed on a Sunday, just before and through midday, during a waxing (new) moon. There should be no-one else in the house.

1 Bless and consecrate yourself, using the Angel Spell. Place the salt in the bowl. Starting in the top right-hand corner of the house, sprinkle a pinch of salt in the four corners of the room, and all corners of every window and door. Proceed clockwise around the house. As you sprinkle repeat:

I cleanse and purify this room of all unnecessary or negative vibrations.

2 Take the rose geranium oil and light the white candle. Again working clockwise around the house, place the candle in the centre of each room. Anoint all doors and windows with a little rose geranium oil as you say the following invocation:

I call upon the Angels of Light and Love to bless this home and all who enter here.

LEFT: *Birch is one of the purifying trees and has long been used to cleanse environments both psychically and physically. Birch twigs were traditionally used annually to beat the bounds of the parish, and are also used for broomsticks, so that as the floor of a house is brushed clean it is also purified by the power of the tree.*

May love, happiness, and harmony prevail.

3 Place the candle in the centre of your living room. Add six drops of rose geranium oil to the lit aromatherapy burner filled with spring water. Sit quietly, visualizing your home filled with the qualities that you desire.

4 Let the candle burn down almost completely. Anoint the candle with rose geranium oil and sprinkle with rice as thanks to the helpful energies, then fold it into the gold fabric. Place the parcel beneath your front door mat or as close to your door as possible saying:

This I place so that all who enter here will be blessed.

5 Leave the parcel undisturbed until the time when you next perform a blessing, when it can be replaced by a new parcel.

Horseshoes

Horsehoes are an ancient symbol of protection, and are traditionally hung on a front door. They are made from iron, a metal sacred to Mars, and therefore they ensure protection and strength for the occupants of the house. A horseshoe should be nailed firmly to the outside of the door, with the open ends upwards, preferably using iron nails.

Angel Spell

This spell can be performed as another way to bless and consecrate yourself, or to help you or those you know in times of vulnerability. You can use this spell without candles and incense, when you feel it is necessary, by just saying the invocation to the Angels. Always remember to thank these mighty beings of light; whether you sense their presence or not, they will be there.

You Will Need

- 2.7 m (9 ft) white cord
- White candle
- Frankincense
- Charcoal
- Charcoal burner

ABOVE: *Conjure up your visualization of the angels slowly, so that you truly "see" them in your mind.*

Blessing Yourself

1 Open your cord circle and place the candle and frankincense in the centre. Facing south, light the candle and the burner. Add the frankincense to the hot charcoal saying:

Lord of Light, this offering I make.

Say the Angelic Invocation. While you say the first line, touch your head, touching your stomach say the second line, touching your left shoulder say the third line, and touching your right shoulder complete the invocation:

**Uriel above me.
Michael beneath me.
Raphael to my left
Gabriel to my right.
By the power of these great Angels, surround me with light.**

Visualize four angels in the four directions. Bow your head and say "Thank you" to each one. Ask them for what you feel you need. This could be humility, an open heart, strength, honesty or another helpful attribute for the task at hand.

2 When your call for assistance is completed, say "Thank you" again. Blow out the candle and close your circle in the usual way.

Blessing Another

1 If someone you know is in need of angelic protection or healing, you can make an Angel Altar. Place a white candle and frankincense within a circle of salt, enclosed with a recent photograph of the person.

2 Light the candle and frankincense. Say the Angelic Invocation, touching the head and relevant parts of the body in the photo and saying his/her name.

ABOVE: *Salt is part of the crystal kingdom and is the blessed representation of the earth. Use salt to purify, consecrate and to protect.*

3 Leave the altar for 24 hours, then remove the circle of salt, gathering it up so that it can be sprinkled on the earth outside (or in a pot of earth).

4 For serious situations, do the blessing every 48 hours until you feel your work is done. Leave the altar for 24 hours then remove the salt, leaving the circle for 24 hours. Repeat the salt circle and invocation and remove the salt after 24 hours.

Spell to Find Lost Objects

This is a visualization spell, in which you imagine a lost object being drawn back to you. Make sure that you are not disturbed or your attention distracted while you are performing it, otherwise you will not be able to focus your energy.

You Will Need

- 20 cm (8 in) wand of hazel
- Honeysuckle oil
- Yellow cloth

Preparation

Cut the wand from a hazel tree, asking permission of the tree first. Cut it gently and say "Thank you". Leave a gift of a lock of your hair.

ABOVE: *A hazel wand increases the magic of spells as well as giving magical protection during a ceremony. A forked hazel twig has long been used for water divining.*

1 Draw a deosil (clockwise) circle around yourself with the hazel wand, saying:

By the powers of Heaven and Earth I cast this sacred circle in the name of love, light, wisdom and truth.

2 Perform the energetic breathing exercise. Anoint your temples, forehead and hands with honeysuckle oil. Sit or stand in the north, facing south and imagine that you are sitting upon a high mountain made of magnetic crystals. You can see for miles in any direction.

3 Visualize yourself opening your hands, so that the palms are facing upwards. Let us say that you have lost your keys. Say the following invocation:

Swift and sure, my keys return to me.

4 Imagine that your keys are being drawn back to you, by the strength of the magnetic mountain. Draw them back with as much willpower and concentrated thought as you can. Note any pictures that come into your mind and from which direction your keys return to your hands in the visualization.

5 To add to the spell's effectiveness, write what you have lost on a piece of paper and pin it up in your house until the object returns. If the lost object is in someone else's possession, he/she should feel compelled to return it quickly. If nothing happens, you can either try again or accept that the item is irretrievable at this time.

6 Say "Thank you" as usual to the energies that have helped you. Close your spell then move your wand widdershins from the end to the beginning of the original circle, saying:

This spell is done.

Store the hazel wand wrapped in a yellow cloth in a sacred space, such as an altar or the cupboard where you keep your blessed and consecrated magical equipment.

ABOVE: *Honeysuckle increases clairvoyant abilities and helps the mind to be receptive. It is linked to Jupiter, the planet of good luck, and so helps to bring about the desired result of finding what you are looking for.*

Spell for Spiritual Connections

This spell is to improve your spiritual understanding, expand perception and increase connectedness to the spirits or beings of light. The six-pointed star is a powerful mystical symbol. Sitting within it, surrounded by violet candles and amethysts, you will feel yourself filled with spiritual light and be able to draw down the qualities bestowed by the Angels.

You Will Need

- Lotus oil
- Rhythmic spiritual drumming music
- Natural sea salt
- 6 violet candles
- 6 amethysts
- Gold candle

1 Bless all of your equipment for this spell. Facing east anoint your head, hands and feet with lotus oil. Play your spiritual drumming music.

2 Draw a six-pointed star in salt around you, made of two equal-sized triangles. The star should be large enough for you to sit in the centre.

3 Sit or stand in the centre of the star and place one of the violet candles on each of the six points, beginning with the point that is nearest to the south. As you light the first candle, say:

O Angel Gabriel, lift my spirit to touch Levanah, to draw down her magic into my heart.

Light the candle to your right, saying:

O Angel Raphael, lift my spirit to touch Kokab that I may draw down his wisdom and truth.

Turn to the next candle and light it, saying:

O Angel Zamael, lift my spirit to touch Madim that I may draw down courage and strength.

Turn to the next candle and light it, saying:

O Angel Cassiel, lift my spirit to touch Shabbathai, that I may draw down understanding and patience.

Turn to the next candle and light it, saying:

O Angel Sachiel, lift my spirit to touch Tzedek that I may draw down righteousness.

Turn to the sixth candle and light it, saying:

O Angel Anael, lift my spirit to touch Nogah that I may draw down love and beauty.

BELOW: *Amethyst is a highly spiritual stone, linked to the crown chakra, the chakra of spirituality and the mind. It is used to increase spirituality and to aid peaceful sleep.*

The Lotus

The lotus flower symbolizes spiritual enlightenment. When linked to the crown chakra, it is known as the thousand-petalled lotus, symbolizing spiritual blossoming to the light.

4 When all the candles are lit, place an amethyst next to each one. Light the gold candle and place it in front of you inside the star, and say:

Mighty Michael, Angel of the Sun, lift my spirit to touch Shemesh that I may be drawn closer and closer to the light of the Divine. This I ask of you, that I may grow ever closer to the truth. Adonai, Lord of Light, Adonai, Adonai.

5 Play the rhythmical drumming music quietly. Sit with your hands open upon your lap and let yourself be filled with the essence of spiritual light for up to 20 minutes.

6 Close your spell by picking up the amethysts then blowing out the candles, starting with the last one you lit and ending with the first.

7 Close your cord circle, saying:

May divine will be done.

Friendship Spell

Perform this spell within a horseshoe shape set inside your magical cord circle. The colour green and the apple are both sacred to Venus, and sweet peas are the traditional flower of friendship.

You Will Need

- 2.7 m (9 ft) white cord
- 7 green candles
- Aromatherapy burner
- Sweet pea aromatherapy oil, diluted in sesame oil
- 5 seeds from a sweet organic apple
- Gold pen
- Natural paper

Environment

Perform this spell on a Friday during a waxing (new) moon.

Preparation

Bathe, and then massage your whole body with diluted sweet pea oil.

ABOVE: *Apples are sacred to Venus. They represent love, beauty and harmony. Share an apple with a lover to ensure a deepening bond.*

1 Open the cord circle. Place the green candles in a horseshoe shape, with the open end facing north and you facing south in front of it.

2 Place the aromatherapy burner in the centre of the horseshoe shape and add seven drops of sweet pea oil. Lay the apple seeds in the centre also. Light the first candle to your left, saying:

Nogah, Nogah, Light of Love, I honour and illuminate your beauty and call upon you to help me today.

3 Light the next candle with the lit one, then put the first candle down. Continue this way until all the candles are lit. Now light the aromatherapy burner.

4 Take the gold pen and write down your wish on the paper as follows:

By the powers of the four directions, above me and below me, within me and without, I call for favour with Anael, I call for friends of the same heart, that joy and celebration shall prevail.

5 Draw the seal of Venus, shown in the picture opposite, above your words. Pick up your wish and burn it in the flames of the last candle that you lit, visualizing as you do so that your wish is being carried to the skies.

6 Blow out the candles widdershins, saying on the last one "So mote it be". Close your circle in the usual way. Take the apple seeds to a prepared site or pot and dedicate them:

Nogah, these apple seeds I plant to honour you and please you. And as they grow, so is my life blessed with joy of friendships new.

Spell for Good Luck

The power of this spell comes from the mighty oak tree, which lives for hundreds of years and is a symbol of strength. You can purchase a spell bag from a New Age shop, but making one yourself will increase the potency of the spell it contains.

You Will Need

- Small amethyst
- Turquoise crystal
- Oak leaves
- Cinquefoil oil
- Sprig of rosemary
- Spell bag

Environment

This spell is to be performed on a Thursday during a full moon. Perform it beneath an oak tree that looks healthy and strong.

Preparation

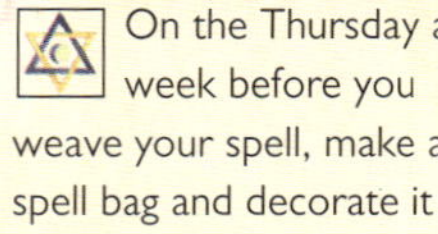
On the Thursday a week before you weave your spell, make a spell bag and decorate it with sequin stars.

To Make a Spell Bag

Any kind of spell bag will do. Make a drawstring bag in this way. You will need: 30 cm (12 in) purple silk, 30 cm (12 in) purple and gold metallic organza, pins, needle and matching sewing thread, paper, pencil, a compass, chalk, cord, masking tape, safety pin, 1.3 m (4¼ ft) gold lace, star and moon sequins and/or beads, 2 gold tassels.

1 Pin and stitch together the two squares of material leaving a 5 cm (2 in) gap along one edge. Trim and turn through. Slip stitch the gap, then top stitch 5cm (2in) from the edge. To make the drawstring, draw a 25 cm (10 in) circle on the paper and cut out. Pin this template to the purple side of the bag and draw round the edge with chalk. Stitch along the line, then stitch another circle, 2 cm (¾ in) further in for the drawstring channel. Fold the bag in half widthways to mark the centre. Cut a small hole through the organza channel at each end of the centre fold. Overstitch the edges to make eyelets.

2 Cut the cord in half and bind the raw ends with masking tape. Fasten a safety pin to the end of one piece and, starting and finishing at one of the eyelets, thread it through the channel. Stitch the two ends together. Thread the other piece in the same way through the other hole.

3 Decorate the bag: slip stitch the gold lace around the outside edge of the bag, sew the sequins on the bag, and attach the tassels.

The Spell

1 Greet your oak tree and tell it your intentions. Place an offering of a small amethyst at its base. Walking deosil in a circle, repeat four times:

O Sachiel, it is I (name). I ask you to hear my call. Light my path, guide my actions, words and deeds and those of all I am yet to meet, that by the power of your might, all will be fortunate to my sight. Good fortune growing, growing, growing, growing.

ABOVE: *The oak is a guardian tree, with great strength and courage. Sacred to the Druids, it is the tree of Jupiter and a fortunate tree to befriend.*

2 Anoint the turquoise crystal and leaves with cinquefoil oil, while visualizing yourself surrounded by the arms of a mighty oak.

3 Place the crystal, the sprig of rosemary and the oak leaves in your spell bag. Hold it up to the oak tree and say:

HEART OF OAK, YOU ARE MY HEART AND WITH HONOUR I SHALL CARRY YOU BY MY SIDE. THANK YOU.

4 Carry your spell with you at all times when you seek good fortune, and store it carefully when not in use.

Spell for the Earth

CHOOSE A PLACE WHERE MANKIND IS USING, OR ABUSING, THE EARTH'S RESOURCES, FOR EXAMPLE A POLLUTED RIVER OR A QUARRY. STAND AS NEAR AS POSSIBLE WITHOUT AROUSING CURIOSITY TO PERFORM THIS SPELL OF ATONEMENT. THE SPELL CAN BE PERFORMED AT ANY TIME.

You Will Need

- Moss agate crystal
- White rose

ABOVE: *Moss agate helps us to communicate with the elemental kingdom, especially when calling for stability on the earth. It is an important stone when performing healing ceremonies for our planet.*

1 Hold the moss agate crystal in your right hand and the rose in your left, and say the following prayer of atonement:

SPIRITS OF THIS PLACE, I COME IN PEACE BUT WITH A HEAVY HEART. I WISH TO SAY HOW SORRY I AM FOR WHAT MY BROTHERS AND SISTERS ARE DOING TO YOU IN THEIR IGNORANCE. I COME TO MAKE AN OFFERING TO SHOW YOU THAT I AM SORRY FOR TAKING FROM YOU WITHOUT RESPECT. I ASK YOUR FORGIVENESS. I ASK YOU TO HELP HUMANITY TO SEE HOW PRECIOUS ALL LIFE IS. I MAKE THIS OFFERING
(Lay down your moss agate)
TO YOU.

2 Transfer the rose to your right hand. Hold it to your heart, say:

CREATOR, GUIDE US ALL IN THE WAYS OF PEACE, LOVE, WISDOM AND TRUTH. I CALL YOU HERE TO (name the place) **TO BRING THE DIVINE TO THIS AREA, TO BLESS IT WITH YOUR HEALING LOVE.**
MAY (name the place) **NOW BE SACRED AGAIN.**

3 Lay down the white rose on the earth. Visualize the whole area filling with white light, embracing it with illumination.

4 If you wish, end the spell with a Native American saying "Mitake Oyassin" (we are all related), or your own personal saying.

Healing Spell

Before you perform this spell, find a suitable tree to bury it under – ash, birch, juniper, orange and cedar trees all have healing powers. Invoke the powers of fresh green lime fruit, to help restore health to yourself or to another person.

You Will Need

- 2.7m (9 ft) white cord
- Gold candle
- Gold pen
- 15 cm (6 in) square of natural paper
- Knife
- Lime
- Gold thread
- 15 cm (6 in) square of orange cloth

Environment

This spell is to be performed on a Sunday.

1 Open the circle and honour the four directions. Light the candle, saying:

Angel Och, I light this flame to honour your presence and ask you to hear this prayer.

2 Write your or another person's name with the gold pen on the paper, at the same time visualizing health and wellbeing surrounding you or them.

3 Cut the lime lengthways into two. Fold the paper three times and place between the two lime halves. Bind the lime halves together with gold thread, saying the following invocation:

Powers of lime,
health is mine/
thine. Cleanse the
body, cleanse
the mind.
Spirit pure, fill
my (or person's)
being with health,
with health,
with health.

4 Place the bound lime in the orange cloth and bind the cloth with gold thread. Close the circle in the usual way.

5 Bury the parcel in the earth, under an ash, birch, juniper, orange or cedar tree. Ask the tree to help you return to good health and thank the tree.

Spell to Stop Gossip

Bury the source of the malicious gossip beneath a holly tree, and ask the tree to protect your good name. The snapdragon is a flower children play with, imagining it can speak as its petals are opened and closed. There is great wisdom in this, as snapdragon is a traditional cure for jaw and throat problems.

You Will Need

- 2.7 m (9 ft) white cord
- Blessed red candle
- Red pen
- A very small square of natural paper
- Snapdragon (*Antirrhinum*) flower
- Thorn
- Red ribbon

Environment

This spell should be performed on a Tuesday, during a waning moon.

Preparation

Find a holly tree to bury your spell under, you might want to perform your spell next to it too.

1 Open your cord circle. Light the red candle, face south and sit down.

2 Write in red pen on the paper square the name of the person or organization that is gossiping about you. If you do not know the name, write "whoever is".

3 Carefully take one of the larger flowers from the stem of the snapdragon and gently open it up. Fold the piece of paper or roll into a tiny scroll and place it inside the flower, repeating five times:

Speak only goodness, think only kind. Look to your own faults and not to mine.

ABOVE: *Holly is sacred to Mars. Use it to call for protection or to banish conflicts.*

4 Keep the scroll of paper in place by sealing the flower head with the thorn, as you do this say:

Flower seal, flower heal lips that speak not from the heart.

5 Take your spell to a holly tree, tell it of your intentions to bury it there and ask its protection over your good name.

6 Bury the snapdragon flower head under the holly tree. Say "Thank you" by tying a small red ribbon to a branch.

7 Leave, visualizing as you walk away, that you are leaving the malicious gossip behind you. Do not look back.

Spell for Removing Conflict

This spell will help remove conflict in a relationship. It will work best if both people in the relationship perform it together. If only one of you wishes to do it, write down what you wish to let go of, don't concern yourself with your partner's reticence and work instead to heal your own difficulties.

You Will Need

- 5.5 m (18 ft) white cord
- A small round table or stool
- 5 red candles
- Charcoal
- Heatproof container
- Coriander seeds
- Red pen
- Two pieces of natural paper

Environment

This spell should be performed on a Tuesday during a waning moon.

1 Open your cord circle. Place the round table or stool in the centre of the circle and on it position the red candles, also in a circle, and light them, remembering which candle is the last to be lit.

2 Light the charcoal in the heatproof container. When it is hot, face west and sprinkle on the coriander seeds, saying:

O Angel Zamael, we call upon you to help us today/tonight, and dedicate this offering to you.

To Make a Wish

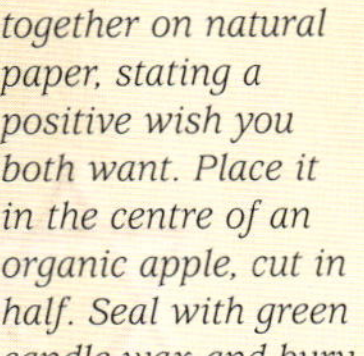

Write your names together on natural paper, stating a positive wish you both want. Place it in the centre of an organic apple, cut in half. Seal with green candle wax and bury it near to the house in a prepared spot. If the apple seeds grow, tend them carefully because they represent new growth in your relationship.

3 Breathe in the aroma of the burning seeds. Each person should then use the red pen to write on their piece of paper the emotion you want to let go of – jealousy, anger, hurt etc.

4 Add your negative feelings to the piece of paper. Then walk widdershins around the table five times, visualizing your emotion and the way you express it.

5 After you have circled the table for the fifth time, each of you should burn your own piece of paper in the flame of the last candle that was lit.

Spell to Sell Your House

Burning frankincense will cleanse your home and purify it of old vibrations, making it ready for the next keeper. A vase of flowers placed in a room on the appropriate day of the week can magically enhance your wishes.

You Will Need

- Frankincense
- Yellow flowers
- Lavender incense
- Front door key
- Yellow ribbon

Environment

This spell is to be performed on a Wednesday, during a waxing (new) moon.

1 Clean and tidy your house thoroughly, then burn frankincense in all the rooms, saying:

Now is time for me/us to leave. With thanks I/we cleanse you.

2 Face west, the direction for letting go. As you say the invocation turn from west to east moving deosil:

I/we let go of this place, so that a new beginning may arise.

3 Place yellow flowers in the living room and burn lavender incense. Tell the house spirit that you wish to depart and need the next keepers to come and take over from you.

The Flowers of the Week

Saturday	evergreens, cypress
Sunday	orange flowers
Monday	white flowers, river plants
Tuesday	red flowers
Wednesday	yellow flowers
Thursday	violet flowers, purple flowers
Friday	pink flowers, roses

4 Hang a front door key from a yellow ribbon in an east-facing window where it can blow in the wind (but not be available for burglars!). Call upon the East Wind to help you move on to new surroundings. As you hang up the key, say:

This property sells, this property sells, here hangs the key to guide the next keeper here.

Spell Tables

These tables can be used to help you develop your own spellweaving skills. By referring to the lunar calendar or planetary tables, you can begin to build a picture of the best times and phases to weave your magic. You will also need an astrological almanac or diary to refer to.

Lunar Calendar

The moon travels through the 12 signs of the zodiac approximately every 28 days, passing through her own four phases during this period. The waxing moon in a sign helps new beginnings, the full moon helps fruitfulness, fertility and increase, the waning moon helps falling away and removing. It is advisable not to weave magic during the deep winter months or during the dark phases of the moon but to reflect, prepare and meditate instead.

♑ **Capricorn**	material matters and concerns, obstacles
♒ **Aquarius**	healing, higher thought, mental health
♓ **Pisces**	psychic work, creative ideas
♈ **Aries**	business, success, innovation, leadership
♉ **Taurus**	material matters, nourishment, physical health
♊ **Gemini**	communication, travel, learning
♋ **Cancer**	family, friends, emotional health, the home
♌ **Leo**	success, wealth, recognition, general health
♍ **Virgo**	harvest, abundance, fruitfulness
♎ **Libra**	balance, harmony, relationships
♏ **Scorpio**	sexuality, occult, ancestors, spiritual understanding, insight
♐ **Sagittarius**	travel, transcendence, wisdom

Planetary Table

This table gives guidelines on which day of the week is best for weaving certain spells, and lists the propitious elements associated with that planet.

Saturday

Saturn

Spellweave on this day to clear obstacles and restrictions.

Minerals	jet, obsidian, lead
Colour	indigo/black
Number	3
Angel	Cassiel
Goddess	Kali
Trees	alder, beech, holly, elm, yew
Plants	ivy, evergreens
Herb	asafoetida
Aroma	cypress

Asafoetida and jet

Sunday

The Sun

Spellweave on this day to attract health, and success and prosperity.

Minerals	topaz, amber, gold
Colour	gold/ orange
Number	6
Angel	Michael
God	Ra-Harachte
Trees	acacia, bay, birch, cedar, walnut, lime, orange, rowan, juniper
Plants	mistletoe, marigold, bay laurel, benzoin gum, angelica
Herb	cinnamon, bay leaves
Aroma	frankincense

Monday

The Moon

Spellweave on this day to increase intuition, perceptions, fertility and all female issues.

Minerals	pearl, moonstone, silver
Colour	silver/blue
Number	9
Angel	Gabriel
Goddess	Selene
Trees	aspen, willow, lemon, eucalyptus
Plants	jasmine, poppy, white lily sea plants, river plants
Herb	sandalwood
Aroma	jasmine

Pearls and lilies

Tuesday

Mars

Spellweave on this day to improve strength, power and authority and to banish conflicts.

Minerals	hematite, ruby, iron
Colour	red
Number	5
Angel	Zamael
Goddess	Anath
Trees	larch, hawthorn, dogwood
Plants	anemone, tobacco
Herb	coriander, garlic, pepper
Aroma	pine

Hematite and garlic

Wednesday

Mercury

Spellweave on this day for all forms of communication, including writing, teaching, speaking, learning, studying, and travel.

Minerals	agate, carnelian, quicksilver
Colour	yellow
Number	8
Angel	Raphael
Goddess	Athena
Trees	ash, hazel
Plants	impatiens
Herb	caraway, lavender, marjoram, dill
Aroma	lavender

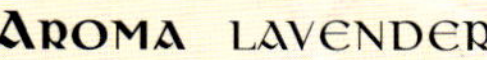

Lavender and agates

Thursday

Jupiter

Spellweave on this day for employment, luck, travel, money, justice and wealth.

Minerals	amethyst, aquamarine, tin
Colour	violet/ purple
Number	4
Angel	Sachiel
Goddess	Juno
Trees	almond, horse chestnut, oak
Plants	avens, honeysuckle
Herb	cinquefoil, nutmeg, sage, anise, cloves
Aroma	honeysuckle

Nutmeg

Friday

Venus

Spellweave on this day for love, friendship, marriage, beauty and harmony and creativity.

Minerals	emerald, jade, copper
Colour	green
Number	7
Angel	Anael
Goddess	Aphrodite
Trees	apple, fig, magnolia, pear, elder, damson,
Plants	heather, Hyacinth, rose, love-in-a-mist, iris, periwinkle, violet
Herb	vervain, myrtle, yarrow
Aroma	rose

Spells and Nature

The high magician works very closely with nature, communing with planets and stars, trees, plants, fairies, devas, angels, animals, stones, crystals and the elements of earth, air, fire and water. Following the circle of life and the wheel of the year, there are many ways to weave a magical nature spell.

Birds and Their Meanings

Any feathers that you find can be used in spellweaving. The birds themselves have particular messages and meanings, and you can use the appropriate feathers for magical spells.

Bird	Meaning
Blackbird	gatekeeper
Crow	change
Duck	love and harmony
Eagle	clarity
Hawk	foresight
Magpie	relationships
Owl	wisdom
Pigeon	messages
Robin	protection
Swan	purity
Woodpecker	magic and prophecy
Wren	protection

Stones and Their Meanings

Stones, crystals and gems are used a great deal in high magic. Here are a few and their meanings to me. Find and work with stones that have particular meaning for you.

Stone	Meaning
Agate	for inspiration from the spiritual realms
Amethyst	mental and spiritual balance
Aquamarine	to increase psychic powers
Citrine	the prosperity stone
Celestite	to link with angels
Flint	psychic protection
Fossil	to link with earth wisdom
Moss agate	earth healing
Seashell	fertility
Smoky quartz	absorbs negative vibrations, grounds and stabilizes
Turquoise	healing and protection
Vanadinite	mental focus, life direction

Trees and Their Meanings

Trees and plants have particular qualities and abilities. This table will help you to choose an appropriate tree according to the spell you are weaving.

Healing spells	ash, aspen, elder, eucalyptus
Spiritual spells	alder, bamboo, pine, witch hazel, yew
Purification spells	bay, birch, broom, cedar, tamarisk, willow
Protection spells	ash, cypress, holly, larch, mulberry, rowan, oak
Fertility spells	banana, birch, fig, hazelnut, oak, pine (cones), walnut, willow
Increase the magic of spells	apple, ash, hazel, rowan, willow, witch hazel
Love spells	apple, apricot, pomegranate, nut, willow
Prosperity spells	almond, horse chestnut

Glossary

Angels:

- **Anael** Angel of the planet Venus
- **Cassiel** Angel of the planet Saturn
- **Gabriel** Angel of the moon
- **Michael** Angel of the sun, the leading angel
- **Och** Healing spirit of the sun
- **Raphael** Angel of the planet Mercury
- **Sachiel** Angel of the planet Jupiter
- **Uriel** Angel of the the north and Earth
- **Zamael** Angel of the planet Mars

Adoni Hebrew name meaning lord of light.

Beltane Celtic May Day fertility festival to mark the beginning of summer.

Chakra Sanskrit word for "wheel", names the body's centres of energy.

Crown chakra Energy centre found at the top of the head.

Deosil To move in a clockwise direction.

Devas A name for beings of the light.

Diana Goddess of fertility, linked to the full moon.

Equinoxes Two fixed points of the year, spring and autumn

Esbats Times of lunar celebration.

Hara The place of inner knowing located in the abdomen.

Imbolc Celtic festival marking spring.

Kokab Hebrew name for the planet Mercury.

Lammas Celtic festival of the harvest.

Levanah Hebrew name for the moon.

Madim Hebrew name for the planet Mars.

Mote Old English word meaning "shall".

Nogah Hebrew name for the planet Venus.

Samhaine Celtic festival, also known as Hallowe'en.

Shabbathai Hebrew name for the planet Saturn.

Shemesh Hebrew name for the sun.

Sigil A pictorial depiction of a name.

Smudging Cleansing, using the smoke of burning herbs.

Solstices Two fixed points of the year, marking midwinter and midsummer.

Tzedek Hebrew name for the planet Jupiter.

Waning The moon's decrease in influence.

Waxing The moon's increase in influence.

Widdershins To move anti-clockwise (counter-clockwise).

Love Charms

For centuries people have been making love charms and performing rituals to enhance their relationships and their fertility. Tales of love charms are woven into the myths and legends of every culture, and show how a spell, song, sacred object or creature strengthens the connection between two people to draw them closer together.

The Nature of Love

To love someone is to give wholeheartedly, without expectation, and to receive openly, without judgement or reservation. Only your true self can love in this way.

When cynicism or ego does not weigh you down, when you are not living in the past or in an imagined future, then you are at peace with yourself and can love. Love represents the heart, not the mind, and it can defy the restrictive boundaries of reason. Love can express raw emotions, uncut and untempered by logic or analysis. It does not exist just to please another or yourself, it simply is.

Love is universal and connects all things. You need only to open your heart to experience the wellspring of love all around you. That connection may be romantic love, filial love, sisterly love or the love for an animal or flower.

Making a love charm and filling it with your hopes, not your fantasies, with your un-conditional love, not your desires, reminds you who you are and where you are going. It is firstly a gift to yourself. Everyone is special, and as you make the charm, it, too, becomes special. It will represent your current thoughts and feelings, and when you give a love charm, you pass on that respect and uniqueness. Giving a love charm is a sign that you truly honour and love that person.

LAURA J WATTS

LEFT: *Love charms can be made from everyday objects you see around you or you can gather together a collection with a charm in mind.*

OPPOSITE: Romeo and Juliet, *1884 by Sir Frank Dicksee (1853–1928).*

Love is patient and kind; love is not jealous or boastful; it is not arrogant or rude. Love does not insist on its own way; it is not irritable or resentful; it does not rejoice at wrong, but rejoices in the right. Love bears all things, believes all things, hopes all things, endures all things.

1 Corinthians, 13 (4–7)

The Art of Giving

To give without expectation is the essence of a love charm. When you give expecting something in return, you do not love wholeheartedly, you love conditionally.

Giving a love charm as a bargain for gratitude, forgiveness or promises is an act of egoism, not of the true self. You are dishonouring yourself, the person to whom you are giving the gift and your relationship.

The joy of giving is never to want anything in return. Making a love charm is an act of unconditional expression. You are creating something that may have the briefest of existences; it may be given and forgotten or it may be treasured for a lifetime. It does not matter which and does not change how valuable the charm is or the intent with which it was made.

The Way to Give

A truthful person should not judge how a person receives a gift. In giving, you speak the truth of your heart and show the recipient your deepest love and honour. You may feel he or she has not heard, may not care, or may not even understand. This is the voice of your ego judging that person's response. In judging another person you show that you no longer trust or believe in him or her.

The making and giving of a love charm must be done with the whole self, which is who you are when you are not dwelling on the past or the future. You must live in each heartbeat, accepting every moment with pleasure.

LEFT: *Flowers have long been a token of love and affection and are given not only to lovers, but also to friends and family.* Tristan and Isolde, *1904 by Andrew Watson Turnball.*

Yesterday's the past and tomorrow's the future. Today is a gift, which is why they call it the present.

Bill Keane

The Art of Receiving

When someone honours you with a gift, he or she reminds you that you are special, that you are unique in this world. You should return that honour and accept the gift with an open heart.

The ego may say that you are not worthy or that you are too proud, but your true self feels the love inherent in the gift and will shine through, if you let it. The gift may be a compliment, a present, a touch or a simple glance. These gifts are offered to your heart so you should let it speak openly in reply.

You should give without expectation or judgement and you should receive gifts in this way. If you are responding honestly, without wanting something in return, then you do not have anything to fear. If you do not judge the gift, whether it is bought or handmade, whether it is large or small, then you see only the intent behind it. All gifts are equal. The difference is in how you perceive them.

Accepting Gifts

A gift is a beautiful thing and should be received with beauty and grace. A love charm captures the beauty in your heart. If you accept a love charm with the deepest honour and respect, so you honour and respect the giver.

Receiving is an art that has been lost to many; people sometimes feel self-conscious when someone pays a compliment, or can be suspicious of an invitation. They often choose to see only the shadows of a person's motives. The cynical voice inside the head drowns out the innocence of the heart. A world full of shadows is a dark place. Let go of your fears and accept with wisdom and not question the intent behind a person's gift. Look for only the light of his or her heart's intentions.

You are given each day as something new to experience. All you must do is accept it for the gift that it is. Gifts also come from people's hearts and fill your everyday life, whether they be simple words, a touch or the offer of food. It is up to you to accept these things and see them for what they truly are, a love charm for your own unique heart.

LEFT: *Gifts do not have to be of material value: gestures and kindnesses are of great value.* The Kiss *by Sir Lawrence Alma-Tadema (1836–1912).*

Legendary Love Charms

Tales of love charms are woven into the myths and legends of every culture, and show how a spell, song, sacred object or creature strengthens the connection between two people to draw them closer together.

In Celtic mythology, the hero, Diarmuid, had a beauty spot on his cheek which enticed Gráinne, the wife of his chief to run away with him. He refused her love until she put a *geasa*, a word of power on him, and he became her lover. The *geasa* is a love charm, a simple word, which if spoken from the heart can give birth to something new and passionate. Words can have the power to bring love to life.

Sometimes your voice is not one of words but one of song. In a Native American Sioux myth, a young, lonely hunter became lost in a forest. As he tried to rest, he heard a beautiful, ghostly sound that made his heart ache, and he was led by a woodpecker to its source. He found a cedar branch full of holes hammered out by the bird, and heard the high, haunting song as the wind blew through it. Reverently, he brought this roughly-made flute back to his people and composed a special song for his *winchinchala*, his sweetheart. Its beautiful sound transfixed her, bringing her to him and she agreed to marry him. The Sioux regard the flute as an instrument for speaking to the heart of a loved one.

Love charms can also symbolize the eternal and spiritual nature of love. According to legend, Tristan, nephew of King Mark of Cornwall, and Iseult, Mark's future Queen, mistakenly drank a love potion intended for the King. They fell deeply in love and for a time the lovers met in secret. The King discovered their affair and Tristan left for voluntary exile in Brittany. Eventually the tragic pair were buried side by side and, above their graves, two yew trees grew so close together that they became entwined. Yew trees regenerate and in many religions they are thought to aid the passing of a soul from death into a new life. Love, like the yew tree, is also part of an eternal cycle of birth, death and rebirth, and only by accepting that cycle will you be able to love forever.

In Greek mythology, the goddess of love, beauty and fertility, Aphrodite, often used

spells and charms to do her mischievous work on the gods and mortals alike. She is an iconic figure, born from the foam of the sea and is often depicted rising from the waves. Her charms often had poor consequences, as she frequently seduced men and exerted her heavenly powers to satisfy her own erotic pleasure, and not her heart. She was said to charm the god of war, Ares, into her bed, but was caught by her husband, Hephaistos. Zeus, the ruler of the gods, punished her infidelity by forcing her to sleep with a mortal.

Cupid was the Roman god of love and the son of Venus, the Roman goddess of love. He was often depicted as a cherubic, but capricious and wanton boy, armed with a quiver full of "arrowed desires" or a torch to inflame love in the hearts of gods and men. Some of his arrows, however, would turn people away from those who fell in love with them.

According to one myth, Venus was jealous of the beautiful mortal, Psyche (Greek for "soul") and told Cupid to make her love the ugliest man alive. But Cupid fell in love with Psyche and hid her in a secret place where he could visit her every night. He told her never to try to see his face, but one night she lit a lamp and saw Cupid beside her. He reproached her and fled, fearing what his mother might do to him now that his secret was discovered. Psyche searched the world for Cupid, until the god Jupiter granted her immortality and gave her in marriage to Cupid.

Love charms have as much potential to do harm as to do good; what goes around, comes around. You should be willing to receive similar vibes to the ones you generate.

OPPOSITE: Tristran and Iseult Drinking the Love Potion, *1867 by Dante Gabriel Rossetti (1828–82).*

LEFT: The Mirror of Venus, *c. 1885 by Edward Burne-Jones (1833–98).*

BELOW: Cupid Delivering Psyche, *1867 by Edward Burne-Jones (1833–98).*

Fairytale Love Charms

The world is rich in allegorical fairytales that speak of the connection a love charm can bring to two people.

In the tale of *Beauty and the Beast*, it was the charm or gift of a rose that brought the two lovers together. A man picked the rose for his daughter, Beauty, but the beast, who owned the rose bush, demanded her life in exchange for the gift. Beauty agreed to live with the beast in his castle and in time came to care for him. One day, she left to see her father, but the beast began to die without her. She rushed back and declared her love for him and in so doing released him from a spell and he became a prince. The rose brought the two lovers together, but it was the words of Beauty that transformed their love and brought it to life.

This act of declaring love, of giving wholeheartedly, is so magical and powerful that fairytales abound with it. The frog-prince was transformed by the kiss of a princess. In the story of *Sleeping Beauty*, she was woken by the kiss of a prince, as she lay surrounded by enchanted rose thorns. By expressing what is in their hearts, everybody has the capability to transform someone else.

The story of Cinderella has many roots. One of them, Grimm's *Aschenputtel*, is a story of how a love charm can motivate someone to fulfil a heart's dream. Aschenputtel planted a hazel twig on her mother's grave. A tree grew and a

dove came to nest there. One day a prince invited her ugly stepsisters and her to three balls. On the first night, she was left behind and she sat under the tree in despair. The dove heard her crying and it fetched her a dress as a gift to wear to the ball. She went to each ball and danced with the prince.

After the third ball, in her rush to get home, she left a slipper behind. The prince visited every house looking for her. Finally he was united with Aschenputtel. The dove was the charm that spoke to her and acted to bring their love together. But it was only because she was looking for love that the dove's message was heard.

A love charm may sound in the smallest moments; you should always try to listen for its call.

The fairytale of Rapunzel tells of how love can heal the deepest wounds. A witch locked Rapunzel in a high tower, but she was visited by a prince who climbed up her long hair to her window. One day, the witch found them together and threw the prince from the window. He fell on to a patch of thorns and was blinded. The witch sent Rapunzel to a land far away. Years later, the prince, who had been blindly wandering, heard her singing, and they were reunited. Rapunzel's tears of joy cascaded into the prince's eyes, healing his lost vision.

OPPOSITE TOP: *From* Beauty and the Beast *by Edmund Dulac (1882–1953).*

OPPOSITE BOTTOM: The Sleeping Beauty *by Thomas Ralph Spence (1855–1918).*

RIGHT: Rapunzel, *1908 by Frank Cadogan Cowper (1877–1958).*

Courting Charms

Many ancient traditions for the giving of love charms have been passed down over the years and still survive today. Some are rituals for courting and marriage; others are part of the timeless quest for a faithful, loving partner.

Whether by insight or by searching, innumerable love charms and rites have always been used to find a true partner and love. Food is especially symbolic in all parts of the world. Fruit, as a rich fertility symbol, has been used often in courting rituals. Many foods have a meaning – it might come from their shape, colour, taste or history. Apples have long been symbolic of love and fertility.

Giving food and the act of cooking for someone you love can be a charm or means of seduction. Baking a cake or cooking a delicious symbolic meal for a person you love is as important today as it was hundreds of years ago.

Wedding cakes have been a symbol of love for centuries and sharing the cake is significant of sharing love. Trees and plants also receive symbolic meaning. Their leaves, the places they grow, the way their branches reach to the sky, can all have some relevance to your lives and love if you see it. Trees led to one of the first ancient alphabets and wood rituals have been used for love charms all over the world. Flowers, too, have a long history as lover's gifts. A "language" of flowers has become popular, and lovers still give flowers on special days.

Tea

As part of the elaborate Chinese courting ritual the man would give the woman and her family *cha-li*, or tea presents. Tea, along with other gifts, such as sugar, wine, tobacco, cake and poultry, was presented and distributed by strict etiquette. Making tea for someone is a common ritual today, but even simple rituals can be important when imparting love.

LEFT: *An intimate meal with the person you love can be a part of a love charming ritual.*

Apple Pips

An apple was once cut in half and the pips counted. An even number of pips would indicate that a new love would lead to a happy marriage. An odd number was a sign that the woman would remain unmarried for some time. If a pip had been cut through, then the love would be stormy and ultimately faithless, if two pips had been cut then the love was doomed to fade.

Beech Bark

Beech bark was the first paper used for writing magical inscriptions. If you found some beech bark or wood, you could use it as part of an ancient wishing spell whereby you would inscribe your wish upon the bark and bury it in the ground. As the bark was consumed by the earth, so the wish would be released into the world and it would begin to show itself in your life.

Hazelnuts

The hazel was believed to be a tree of knowledge and wisdom. Hazelnuts were revered as the food of gods. At Hallowe'en, a lover could take two hazelnuts, one for each person, and throw them into a fire. If they lay there quietly side by side, the match was deemed faithful, but if one nut moved away from the other, it was believed that one of the pair was unfaithful at heart.

Birch Garland

Birch is a tree symbolizing the birth of something new. In pagan times, silver birch was especially revered as a tree of feminine creation and wisdom. A Welsh ritual called for a man to weave a garland of birch wood and leaves and give it to the woman he loved. If she reciprocated his feelings, she would return the favour and present him with a garland. The garlands were a pledge of their love.

Marriage Charms

There are many different marriage charms and gifts exchanged between men and women across the world to symbolize commitment. The tradition of giving tokens of love to one another in a marriage ritual has existed for centuries and the objects exchanged are deeply significant.

Rings

The giving of a ring to symbolize a marriage bond derives from the Anglo-Saxon ceremony where a woman transferred her lands to a house-man, or husband. The man would hand the woman a ring along with his wealth and declare that he would worship and honour her. The wife would then accept the ring, as a token of their eternal union, and agree to the familiar vows, including the now unused phrase, "to be bonny and buxom in bed". The marriage ceremonies of many cultures include the giving or exchange of rings and other items of jewellery, but the type of wedding ring and finger on which it is worn varies.

Lock of Hair

Hair is a deeply personal and expressive part of your body. Ownership of a person's hair was considered to impart a magic bond between two people. In Ireland, a man would offer a woman he loved a woven bracelet of hair, which, if she accepted, symbolized their permanent connection. In more recent times a lock of a lover's hair, curled into a circle, would be kept in a love locket. The circle of hair, like the woven hair bracelet, indicated a love that was eternal and timeless. This attitude sentimentally manifested itself in the custom of a widow's mourning jewellery made from the hair of her dead husband.

Jumping the Broomstick

The custom of jumping the broomstick goes back many hundreds of years. A man and woman would take each other's hands in front of a witness, their grasp forming the symbol of eternity. They were said to be handfasted, married for a year and a day. The couple then jumped over a broomstick made of birch twigs. The birch symbolized the letting go of the past and the bringing in of the new.

This was considered "common-law" marriage and was a popular marriage custom in Britain until, in the 16th century, the Church legalized marriage ceremonies, but only those conducted by a priest.

Symbolic Squash

In the Slavic region, a man wanting to propose properly to a woman would present her with an earthenware pot containing squash. The pot was a sign of permanence and would be displayed over her hearth, should she welcome his courtship. The squash were symbols of love and fertility. Each squash was decorated with polished stones, a work of craftsmanship performed by the man for his love. If the woman consented to be his wife, the stones would become part of a wedding anklet, which was the symbol of her status as a married woman. This elaborate decoration of food is a powerful love charm.

Tokens for Love Charms

There are many symbols and objects that can be used when making love charms. Symbols of the earth include trees, animals, flowers and stones, while symbols of the soul include words and letters, patterns and pictures, and body and motion.

Trees

The language of trees, their unique characteristics and symbolism, have always been a part of charms and ceremonies. By walking through a forest and noticing how each tree is different, you can find something that speaks to your heart personally. The wood, bark, leaves or fruit of a tree can be used in creating an individual love charm.

Love Ritual

Find a space outdoors where you feel at peace with yourself. Look at any trees around you. Notice how unique each one is. See if a tree catches your attention and gather a fallen branch or twig from it. Use the branch as a talisman to remind you of the tree and that special place.

Apple Tree

The apple tree is a symbol of love and peace. Offering an apple or apple blossom is a display of timeless love. The Norse goddess, Iduna, and the Greek god, Apollo, both protected an apple tree laden with the golden fruit of immortality and youth. Apple wood can be carved into amulets and talismans for love and longevity. Apple blossom was scattered to mark a place as sacred to love.

Willow Tree

The willow bends easily to the wind; it is a tree of forgiveness and acceptance, of balance and flexibility. You need all of these as you walk the path of a loving relationship. Willow is a great healer; its bark contains the same ingredients as aspirin. Willow often grows by rivers and streams; water cleanses you, washes off the past and helps to heal old wounds.

Holly Tree

The holly is a guardian tree. Its sharp, spiky leaves protect its red berries. Mistletoe is often found growing close to holly in mid-winter and the two plants together symbolize male and female fertility. Weaving a garland of holly and mistletoe is still a custom at Yuletide today, allowing the male and female to become entangled in an unbroken circle.

FLOWERS

These are beautiful and transitory. They are a symbol of opening, awakening and passion. Through its colour, a flower calls out to be pollinated, to join with its fertile partner. We give flowers to call out to one another, to speak our hearts to people. Oils from flowers, such as camomile, jasmine and lavender, can be used for wonderful aromatic love charms. Aromatherapy massages, baths and perfumes can be a simple, direct expression of the heart.

LOVE RITUAL

TAKE THE TIME TO SMELL THE SCENT OF THE FLOWERS AROUND YOU. NOTICE WHAT EACH SCENT BRINGS TO MIND: A MEMORY OR A SENSATION. FIND A SCENT THAT REMINDS YOU OF SOMETHING JOYFUL, AND PLACE A BUNCH OF THOSE FLOWERS SOMEWHERE SPECIAL IN YOUR HOME.

ROSE

This is a timeless symbol of love and regeneration. The first red rose was supposed to come from the blood of Aphrodite, the Greek goddess of love, who trod on a white rose and bled. Death symbolized by a white rose can lead to new life and love (the red rose). The thorns of the rose and its blood-red colour are reminders of the pain of being reborn. Letting go of the past is a difficult but necessary part of opening the heart to the possibility of new love to come. The rose can be a token of accepting love unconditionally.

LILY

The lily gives off a pungent perfume that can stimulate the heart. The white flowers are symbolic of purity, peace and innocence. It was said that lilies grew up where drops of milk from the earth goddess, Hera, fell to the ground when she created the Milky Way. The lily was sacred to the ancient eastern goddess, Astarte, symbolizing the rebirth of love and life at that time of year. The lily can bring a return to innocence and peace after a storm. It is a reminder that mistakes offer a chance to learn and be renewed.

ABOVE: *Roses and other flowers have been the gifts of lovers for thousands of years.*

Animals

The animal kingdom was considered to be wise and a source of guidance and understanding. An animal can touch our spirits. Particular animals may already have a meaning for you, for example, a bird that is nesting nearby or the memory of a dolphin at sea. What you feel and associate with those moments can help you find what you are looking for.

Love Ritual

Notice what animals or insects are living close to you. Is there one that you see often nearby?
Watch the way it moves. Listen to hear if it has a song.
See if there is something that uplifts you and share that feeling with someone you love.

Dove

The dove is not only an image of peace and love, but also of rebirth. Dove feathers can be used in love charms. The gypsy people believed that the dove represented woman and the serpent represented man, and that together they brought new life. The dove was sacred to Aphrodite in her role as a bringer of death and new love, and it was a dove that told Noah that new life could begin after the Great Flood.

Seal

These abound in Celtic mythology, such as the Selkie who came ashore on certain nights and shed their skins to become beautiful women until they returned to the ocean at dawn. They are symbols of change, of the wisdom that comes from within, and reminders that to live with love and beauty you must accept and celebrate that the person you love, as well as you, will constantly change.

Swan

The white swan is a divine bird, closely associated with purity, love and amorousness. The fierce Norse Valkyries wore magical, swan-feather cloaks during their rides from Valhalla. Brahma and Zeus were reincarnated into a swan to give birth to the world. The swan is a symbol of transformation. By accepting the transformation of love you can accept and respond to its passion.

Stones

Rocks and stones are formed under great stress and earthly forces. Each stone on a beach is different; some appear to have faces or animals staring out from them. Giving a stone as a love charm is an ancient ritual. A stone from your garden can be as special as one set in an engagement ring.

Love Ritual

GO FOR A WALK AND LOOK AT THE STONES THAT YOU PASS, WHETHER THEY ARE ON A GRAVEL PATH, IN A WALL OR ON A BEACH. SEE IF YOU CAN NOTICE A FACE ON THE STONE. IF YOU SEE ONE, THINK OF WHOSE FACE IT REMINDS YOU OF. PICK IT UP, IF YOU CAN, AND GIVE IT TO THE PERSON YOU LOVE. TELL HIM OR HER WHAT IT MEANS TO YOU.

Diamond

Literally translated from Latin, diamond means world goddess. It is the hardest mineral substance known on Earth and was said to rule all other stones. In Tibet, the World Goddess was reincarnated as a diamond and this association with a virgin goddess developed into its symbolism as a new beginning. It is also a symbol of indestructible love.

Ruby

The ruby's rich deep-red, rose, carmine or even purple colour symbolizes vitality and passionate love. Its richness was thought to overcome illness and disease by cleansing the wearer of negative emotions and feelings. The ruby is a stone of passion, raising feelings and thoughts from fear and sadness to love and joy.

Pearl

The shimmering pearl and its spherical shape is associated with the cycle of the moon and with the circle of eternity. It was believed that a pearl was formed when lightning struck the eye of a shellfish. Lightning is a powerful symbol of wisdom from the sky, and pearls are a sign of knowledge and understanding. It is also a symbol of perfection.

ABOVE: *Cut or uncut rubies used in love charms are symbols of passion.*

Words and Letters

Writing or carving symbols and words was considered sacred and extremely powerful by many old cultures. When you hold a word or symbol in your mind and commit that permanently into the world by transcribing it, you are transferring your thoughts into reality. Inscribing a special mark, word or phrase into an object can help you to communicate your dreams to the world and, by destroying that object, allow you to let go of past dreams.

Love Ritual

Think of a phrase, a line in a poem or a saying that has some personal meaning for you. Take the first letter of each word and spend some time arranging them on a page. Create a pattern with the letters, perhaps linking them in a circle.

ABOVE: *This inscription on this bindrune means "to gain inspiration".*

Runes

The Norse runic alphabet has many letters which can be combined together to create a single symbol. Each letter had some deep significance, which was used for divination as much as writing. For example, *Ansuz*, or mouth, is the letter for speaking and communicating. *Gyfu* is the letter for giving: its cross shape symbolizes the connection between two people. *Beorc* is the rune for new beginnings. Other runes that may be useful in creating a love charm are given in the Table of Symbols.

Inscription

Inscribing words or a phrase, or even just a date, on to an object is a wonderful way to endow that object with memories and dreams. It has always been common for jewellery, when given as a gift, to be inscribed with secret words or a poem which would be understood only by the wearer. Any gift can be made unique by writing, carving, painting, or stitching on it some words of special meaning. The words can transform any object into a symbol of love.

Monogram

Taking the initials of two people's names and drawing those letters entwined together symbolizes their union. Spend some time designing a monogram for your relationship. Let your feelings express themselves freely in the contours of the letters. Consider all the unique ways in which your two lives overlap and shape those into the monogram. Creating something that uniquely defines your relationship is a symbol of your active intent to entwine your two lives together.

Patterns and Pictures

The image and its associated meaning contained within a picture or pattern can sometimes communicate something deep inside you. A landscape from a holiday, a sunset on a beach, or the wings of a butterfly can all have deep significance. Pictures have been used to express feelings throughout history. Giving a picture as a symbol of the journey you are sharing with someone is a profound way of honouring your path together.

Love Ritual

FIND SEVERAL OBJECTS THAT ARE IMPORTANT TO YOU. ARRANGE THEM TOGETHER IN ANY WAY UNDER A LIGHT OR IN THE SUN AND THEN LOOK AT THE SHADOWS THAT THEY MAKE. DRAW THE OUTLINE OF A PART OF THE SHADOW TO MAKE A PATTERN. THIS PATTERN IS A SYMBOL OF ALL THE MEANINGS OF THOSE SPECIAL OBJECTS.

Shapes

The outline of a shape, the number of its sides and its colour can have special significance if you choose. The perfect symmetry of a circle is a timeless symbol of eternity. The crescent moon and its thirteen phases is a symbol of balance: light against dark, reminding us that all things wax and wane naturally. The three sides and points of a triangle represent the three aspects to life and a living relationship – youth, maturity and learned wisdom. The five-pointed star speaks of brightness and passion. The square is a symbol of equality and strength.

Knots

The Celts used a sacred love knot to tie two people together. It was said to cast a spell over the lovers until the knot was untied. The intricate designs of the Celtic knot are never-ending lines, symbolizing the eternal nature of life and love. The Celts often used animals in imagery, their mouths holding their tails, creating a design of writhing creatures. Weaving a pattern using two threads is a sign of sharing your path with someone. Folktales from all over the world tell of how a woman seeks to bind her lover by tying knots in a possession, such as a riding whip or girdle.

ABOVE: *A Celtic triple spiral symbolizing love, marriage and birth has a never-ending quality.*

Body and Motion

The way you move your body speaks more intuitively and honestly of your actions, thoughts and feelings than any symbol. Your touch, the way you smile and the rhythm of your dance are the truest symbols of your feelings. Your body is a doorway through which you express your soul, your fears, your hopes and your love.

Love Ritual

When you are with someone you care about, ask him or her if they would like a hug. If he or she accepts, hug him or her with your heart beating against one anothers. In those moments, think about how you feel about that person and try to let your body express those thoughts. A hug is a wonderful gift of joy, compassion and love.

ABOVE: *Music and rhythm have made people dance and express their feelings since the earliest times.*

Dance

When you move your body in time and in step with the person you love, you are communicating on the deepest level. Many cultures see dance as the doorway to wisdom and knowledge. If you let go and give yourself to the dance, if you forget about performing in front of other people or behaving for someone else and let every muscle respond, you are letting your body naturally call out to your soulmate. Your soulmate is a person who can understand your dance and the expression of your body, and respond to you intuitively.

Touch

The magical gift of touch, the sensation of another body pressing its warmth against your own, is profound. The touch of a person's hand can open something deep inside you. Often, the touch of another can help you to release something. Touching someone can be both healing and sensual, such as when giving a massage. Touch offers comfort and reminds you that you are not alone – it can make you feel wanted, needed and that you are part of the world, whether a tribe, a culture, or a family – and always a part of the Earth.

Seasons and Cycles

Different times of the year had huge symbolism for couples in the past. Each season was linked to life shared with the land. Even today, our bodies respond to the light and the temperature outside, so that we tend to be reflective by the fire in winter and active in the sun in summer. Other cycles are equally important, such as a woman's menstrual cycle, which ebbs and flows with the moon. Choosing a time to give a love charm within these cycles can give it another level of significance.

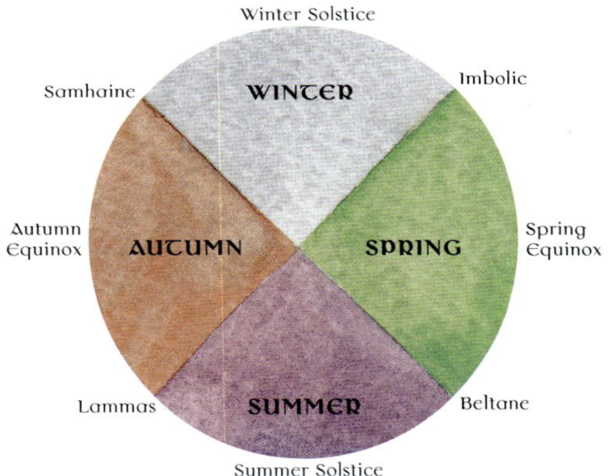

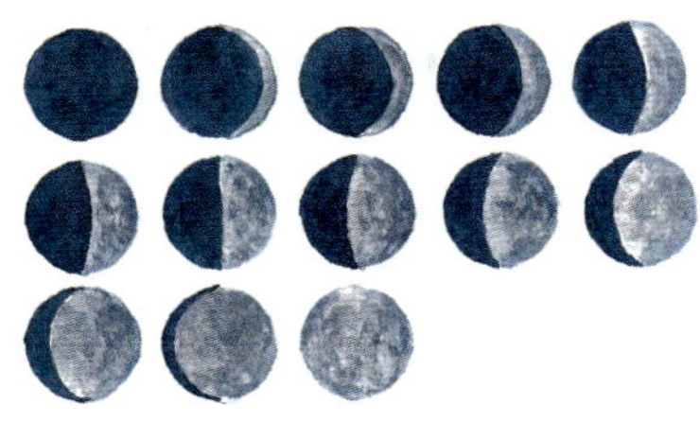

ABOVE: *The thirteen stages of the moon, from no moon to full moon.*

Wheel of the Year

The Celts believed that all things begin in darkness, in winter, which is a time for letting go of the old and welcoming in the new. It is a time of accepting the past, a time of forgiveness and a time for wounds to be healed. In winter, you dream of the year to come. Spring comes with the leaves. It is the season of awakening and preparation and when you express the dreams of winter. May Day, at the end of spring, was the traditional day to be married. In summer and the time of passion, you reap what you have sown in spring. Then, during the embers of autumn you reach a peace with all those around you, become fulfilled and let go of the dreams of the past to begin the cycle again as winter approaches once more.

Thirteen Moons

A woman's menstrual cycle has always been closely connected with the waxing and waning of the moon. It takes 13 nights for the moon to grow from new to full, which gave the number 13 its auspicious reputation, and the full 26 days is the length of a menstrual cycle. At the full moon, a woman is often ovulating and at her most fertile; this is a time of new beginnings when her body might become filled with life. The new moon, the dark moon, was considered by the Celts a time of death and rebirth; it was often when a woman would withdraw to begin menstruating during her "moon time". This is a time of powerful initiation, wisdom and learning. In many cultures the moon goddess protects lovers.

Love Ritual

During the morning, write down your dreams for the day ahead; perhaps these are things you would like to share with someone you love. Put it to one side. In the evening, read your list of dreams and remember those that you made come true during the day and those that never happened. Forget about all of them, let them go, and focus on the moment you have there and then.

THE CYCLE OF LOVE

The art of giving a love charm is that of listening, both to yourself and to the person you are giving to. You must always be aware of the intent with which you are filling the charm, so that you are always giving from the deepest part of your heart and not from the demands of your ego.

The word charm stems from the Latin word for spell or song, *carmen*. The Roman goddess, Carmenta was known for her words of power and was credited with adapting the Greek alphabet for use with Latin.

A charm was a song or incantation sung by a woman to exert her power, the power of words and love, over a man. Love songs and ballads remain extremely popular and are still sung to give messages of love to someone special. To charm your lover was to spellbind him and cause him to feel lovesick and to act more passionately. Love charms were associated with enchantment and the weaving of love between two people. To give a love charm is the art of expressing yourself towards another, to charm him. Love charms are also an opportunity for you to express the changes and challenges that you face in love. It is a chance for you to look more closely within yourself for an answer to the problems that may lie before you and present them to the person we love. In a bustling world, love charms are a symbol of gentler thoughts and a reminder of feelings that you may have forgotten to show in your life and to the people around you.

Love has always been considered an act of nature, a source of irrational behaviour, as when people feel irrevocably drawn together or suffer love sickness. Just think of some of the common expressions of irrationality that people use: to be mad about someone, blindly in love, thinks the world of, love to distraction, swept off one's feet, and even worships the ground he or she walks on.

These feelings are all part of a cycle of love, around which you are drawn. Love can open you up to new possibilities and new dreams. You are always changed by its touch on your life.

ABOVE: *Relationships can be in constant state of flux. By communicating your feelings and remaining close, you can adapt to changes.*

Wheel of Love

Love is always in Motion. It is always changing and you are drawn around its cycle of growing and learning. To love deeply is to accept that each moment you share in love is transitory, and that the next will bring something new. Love charms can help you flow around that cycle, help you give and forgive, love and be loved.

Love is a natural part of the world and, as with the Wheel of the Year, you can think of the Cycle of Love as a wheel with four seasons.

The Season of Dreams is the start, the time when you are alone or feeling disconnected from your life. This is the time you focus on the dreams of love to come and what needs to change to bring that about. Then, as love begins to flourish and open again, you enter the Season of Hope, the hope that your dreams are being fulfilled. This is the time of innocence and gentleness, moving slowly and carefully as your love deepens. Next comes the Season of Passion. Now you have opened yourself out completely to the other person and feel safe to express your love from every pore of your body. When passion peaks and balances and you find that new possibilities have opened up and that you have been changed by your love, this is the Season of Fulfilment. Now is the time that love heals and renews you until you find you must let go of your old dreams and begin to dream again.

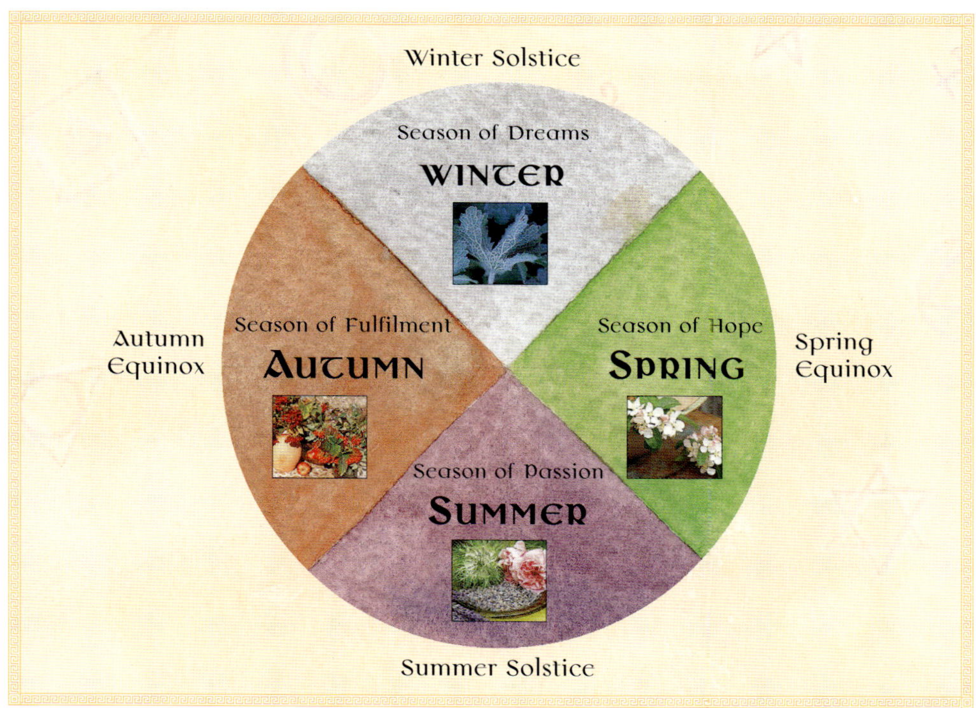

Season of Dreams

This is a time of beginnings, when you pause for a moment and consider where you want to be going and where you have been. What were your dreams? What are your dreams now?

This can be a time when you are alone, or a time when you realize that love has changed you. It is time to reassess your relationships and yourself.

In the Season of Dreams it is dark and you may feel frightened, angry or impatient for something brighter and better to come along. However, in the darkness, you have an opportunity to imagine something completely new and different, to branch out in a new direction. Dreams are your guide – you can map them, follow them and they will lead you to the inner voice of your heart.

This is often a season of frustration, when you find that life is a little harder on you. You must find space in your life for yourself, get to know what makes you happy, what makes you sad, the daydreams you have, and the nightmares. All these dreams are voices from your heart telling you what you want next and what must heal before you can take the steps towards your goal.

It is a time for taking stock of the lessons learned, using them to guide you in what you need next in life, whether it is a new love or the rekindling and transformation of an old love.

As with winter, it is a period of stillness and of waiting and of listening. This is a good time to be alone, even for just a short while, to notice how you feel in your life and your heart. Love charms, as a path for finding your true inner self which may have become muffled in the day-to-day of your life, or drowned in recent pain, will help you. These quiet, contemplative love charms are tokens of the dreams that you are forming for the future and for what has happened in the past that you must now relinquish.

LEFT: *In the Season of Dreams, as with winter, it is a good time to take stock, think and prepare for the coming regeneration of spring.*

OPPOSITE: *Look inwards and examine your relationships.*

Dreams take you on a journey through your consciousness and desires, and help you discover what you need in your life to find love and happiness. Your dreams are the calling of your heart.

Preparation

During the Season of Dreams you need to focus on your own needs and dreams, since you cannot make another person happy without being happy yourself.

Keep a notepad by your bed and write down any dreams you remember. Think about what they mean to you and what feelings they evoke. If they are dreams of seeking out something, think about what you were seeking. If it was a nightmare, were you being chased, and if so, by what and why did it make you afraid?

Note your daydreams too, events from the past which you miss, or possibilities for the future which you yearn for. Find some time alone and sit and imagine that the world is about to end in a few days. Think about it seriously (no one knows what will happen in the future). What would you want to see, to create, to be or do before that happened? What is it that you have always dreamed of but never been able to do? What are the unspoken dreams you carry with you? If they are simple, or even if they seem impossible, write them down.

Now gather up all those dreams and feelings and think. Which are the most important to you? Which ones make your heart beat faster? Which ones would make you feel happy? Which ones would you want to share with someone you love? Which ones would you want to do alone?

All these dreams could be possibilities that you can make happen. Each one could become true if you want it to; it is only a matter of accepting the consequences each might bring and learning from the mistakes along the way. Everyone possesses the power to make changes in their lives and, by imagining their dreams, they take that small step towards being truly happy within themselves.

These are your dreams for the coming cycle.

LEFT: *Try to remember your dreams on waking and think of what they mean. Keeping a notebook by the bed reminds you to write them down while they are fresh in your mind.*

Meditation

This meditation is for clearing the mind of day-to-day worries, allowing you to focus on your inner voice. Once you can quieten your mind, you can easily notice the dreams and needs of your heart and express them in a charm. This may take some practice and you may be surprised at how loud and busy your mind is. Once you master this, do it with your eyes open, so that you can clear your mind, no matter what the distraction.

1 Sit cross-legged with your back straight, head up and your hands loosely clasped and relaxed in front of you. It should not feel too comfortable. Start with your eyes closed. Notice and recognize the thoughts in your mind, the background noises, any other sounds and the smells around you. Now, as each thought comes into your mind, let it go again – do not allow yourself to dwell on anything. Let your thoughts become tranquil and gradually allow your mind to become empty.

2 Breathe in slowly and count your first breath. Do not let your mind wander; focus on your body and the moment. Breathe out slowly. Count ten slow breaths like this, just being and breathing in the moment with no thought of the past or future. Let yourself focus totally on the present and allow the clutter of your mind to fade into silence.

Dream Catcher Love Charm

A dream catcher is a Native American charm for capturing good, wise dreams and for letting bad dreams pass through and away into the night. This is a love charm for awakening the dreams both you and the person you love hold inside your hearts.

Traditionally, a dream catcher is hung above a sleeping person's head, to keep wise dreams so that they can be remembered on waking and so that bad dreams can be forgotten. When you give your love charm, offer to help him or her hang it up and explain your intentions behind the gift. You could also spend some time listening to his or her dreams and sharing your own with your love.

If this is a time of calling love into your life, hang the dream catcher above your bed and listen to your dreams.

Spend a moment considering the wood or tree you want to use for the dream catcher. Also think about what colour ribbon and wool (yarn) you feel would be most appropriate in the charm. Gather feathers that come across your path on a walk or at home, for example.

The dream catcher has a single thread that is wound in a spiral from the outside to the centre, symbolizing the journey from the waking world to the world of dreams. The Native Americans believe that their dreaming selves pass through the heart of a dream catcher and return with knowledge of the dreams of their true selves.

You will need

Fallen branch
Knife
Ball of coloured wool (yarn)
Ribbon
Feathers

LEFT: *The dream catcher is a charm to call in all the deepest dreams and desires of one's heart. It is a gift symbolizing the awakening of a person's heart and your willingness to follow his or her dream.*

1 Find a long, flexible branch from the place you choose and bend it into a circle. You may find you need to trim nodules and smooth the bark.

2 Slice across the branch at both ends so that they lie flat against each other. Secure the ends together using coloured wool (yarn).

3 Cover the circle with ribbon and fasten it securely at one end. This forms the simple outer loop of the dream catcher.

4 Tie the wool to the circle and wind it around the circle a few centimetres (inches) away, not too tautly. Repeat at equal distances around the circle. This is the spiral of thread that weaves into the centre.

5 When you have almost completed the circle, wind the wool around the centre of the next wool span. Repeat this spiral structure until you have a small central circle and then tie off the wool end.

6 Use the wool to secure feathers to your charm. They can be tied either to the branch so that they hang down from the dream catcher, or secured to a wool span, perhaps at the centre. Think about the person this is intended for and follow your instincts.

Dream Space Love Charm

This is a charm that creates a special place for love to rest. It is a place that reminds someone of all the wonderful dreams that love has and will fulfil.

At this time, in the season of dreams, you need to remember what has happened in your life, good and bad, and create new dreams to share with someone. A dream space is a shrine to the past and is also dedicated to the future of a relationship. It is a physical space that you give over to your dreams, as a step towards your dreams physically manifesting themselves in your life. Think carefully about hte place where you want to create the dream space. It should be somewhere you share with the person you love, perhaps even a place outdoors.

Present the dream space love charm and all its intentions to the person you love. Light a candle with him or her in front of the pattern you have created. Spend some time thinking and talking about those dreams. Think about what steps you might have to take to make them come true. Whenever you feel the need, come back to the dream space, light the candle and recall your dream. Remember the steps you must take to get there and how far along the path you have come.

You will need

Picture of a special place or person
Stones
Any other special items from a relationship (such as jewellery)
Candles

1 Find a picture that signifies something both of you dream of, something you want to share together in the future, such as a place you want to travel to or a person you want to see. Think of dreams you have already shared together, and any special items you already have from those dreams. Gather some stones from a special place and focus on the future you want to create with that person.

2 Place the stones around the picture in a shape or pattern that you feel represents your dreams. This may be a circle representing the eternal bond you share, or perhaps a star for the passion that you feel needs to enter into your life. Choose whatever shape feels right for you. Experiment with the pattern until it feels right. Add your other special items.

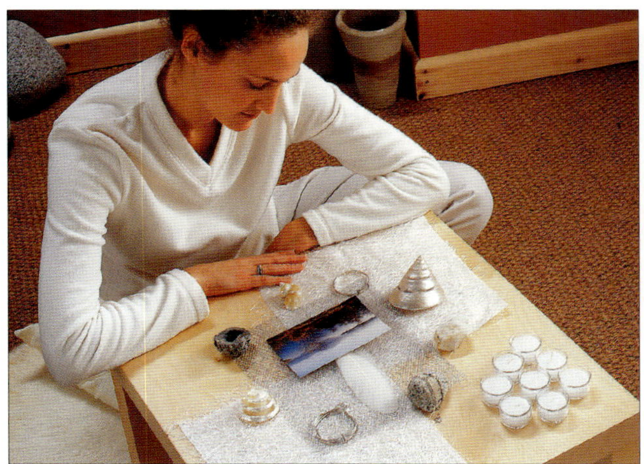

3 If you have a special item that links with the picture, you could place it above or below the picture, if you wish. Spend time focusing where you want the picture.

4 Place the candles around the space, arranging them in a way you feel is appropriate. Remember never to leave burning candles unattended.

Season of Hope

In the Season of Hope new love is beginning to blossom. In the Season of Dreams you demonstrated your intention for change in your life and now something has been kindled, or resurrected, or it has simply altered its course towards your dream. It is a gentle time, where you must be patient and let the love grow slowly and delicately. It is not a time to rush into things but to realize the beauty and wonder of the love that has entered into your life.

During the Season of Hope you may be treasure-hunting – listening and watching for the signs in yourself and in others that love is entering your life. You must turn over every rock, watch for every clue that may lead you to your heart's desire. The world is beckoning you onwards to fulfil your dreams; remain alert to heed its call. Be persistent, be joyful in your search; everything comes to those who wait. Soon, love will appear quietly and completely, enveloping your life.

Now you can begin to touch, smell and taste love around you; it fills your senses. Now is the time to respond to it with all your heart, openly without cynicism, without idealizing it, remembering that it, too, is transitory and will change.

What you do in the Season of Hope is the first step towards realizing the dreams that you experienced in the time before. You must keep in mind where you want to be and celebrate the first uncertain steps without getting waylaid on your journey by the heady feelings that love brings you. You are sowing the seeds of your hopes.

LEFT: *In the Season of Hope, as with spring and new growth, you should gently open your heart to the love that surrounds you.*

OPPOSITE: *Look deeply into your partner's eyes and listen to his or her heart.*

Love, when it is fresh, fills and feeds your soul and allows you to be innocent for a while, enraptured by the pulse of your heart. You hope, against hope, that this is in answer to your dreams and that this will take you to where you want to be. It is the nature of love to hope, and this is the season to believe and to act to fulfil that hope.

Preparation

Spend some time thinking about all the things that you would like to share with the person you love, the things that you have dreamed of that you would like to happen.

Think about what the person in your life has said during the day, such as what he told you about himself or what has been discussed. Did you listen to his needs? Did you truly understand the meaning? In this season people often become caught up in the whirl of love and misunderstand each other, or they may become disconnected from reality and exist in a dream world. You must make the effort to move away from dreaming into the world that exists about you, even if it is sometimes harsh. This is a season of listening.

Here you are laying the seeds for the future. You are setting the boundaries, the expectations of the burgeoning relationship. If you do not hear what the other person dreams of, if you do not hear his thoughts, then you will never know whether the path that you walk will take you closer to or further away from that person. Only by listening to what the other person's ideas and needs, are you able truly to give your heart to him. Later in the relationship you will be able to listen more easily, but now you need to be careful and patient.

Meditation

This is a meditation for listening and looking, reminding you that there is always more to see. You will never see all there is to see on a beach, in a tree or in a person. You must always be looking harder because there is something extraordinary hidden in every tiny crevice and even in the darkest corners.

1 Kneel, sitting on your heels, with your toes behind you and your back and neck straight. Rest your hands on your thighs or knees. This should feel relatively comfortable. Close your eyes and breathe slowly. Relax and try to empty your mind. Start by listening to the noises around you. Try to pick out each distinguishing sound. Listen harder. What background sounds can you notice? Perhaps there are some which you were not even aware of before.

2 Now take three slow breaths and empty your mind again. Open your eyes and look in front of you. Do not move your head, just see what is in front of your eyes. Look closer and notice the textures, the shadows and the patterns hiding even in a simple wall. Take three slow breaths and empty your mind before moving. You can repeat this mental exercise while eating, noticing all the tastes in each mouthful of food, or while dressing, noticing all the textures as they brush against your skin.

Maypole Love Charm

This is an ancient sign of fertility and the joining of the male and female together. People danced around the maypole during the spring May Day festival, with children interweaving coloured ribbons, symbolizing the interwoven nature of man and woman.

This love charm is a symbol of the beginning and hope of spring. Make this small version as a love token to signify the hope that the lives of you and your loved one will be interlinked in the coming cycle. This charm demonstrates your intention to work together with the other person, to weave your paths together, so that both your dreams are fulfilled.

You will need

- Straight wooden stick
- Knife
- Four coloured ribbons
- Thread or wool (yarn)
- Beads, pendants or stones for decoration

ABOVE: *Select ribbons that are appropriate for the person who will receive the maypole. The maypole is symbolic of lives entwining.*

LEFT: *The Maying festival has been enjoyed for centuries.* Come Join in the Maypole Dance *by Henry John Yeend King (1855–1924).*

1 Think about the wood you want to use for the Maypole and then find a fallen branch from a tree. A relatively straight stick will be easier to weave around. Smooth the wood, either by cutting off the nodules or by stripping off the bark. Select four coloured ribbons, keeping in mind the person you intend to give this to. Each ribbon can also represent a season in the cycle of love.

2 Take the lengths of ribbon and secure them around the top of the stick using the thread or wool (yarn). Hold the stick firmly in place and lay out the ribbons in the four directions. You will want to wind the north and south ribbons clockwise and the east and west ribbons anti-clockwise around the wood.

3 Weave two sets of adjacent ribbons together as shown; north ribbon over the west one and the south ribbon over the east one.

4 Repeat weaving the ribbons around the stick crossing alternate, adjacent pairs, in a continuous pattern until you reach the base.

5 Secure the ends with thread or wool. Now, either leave the ribbon ends free, or tie beads, pendants or stones into them to make the charm a unique and special gift.

Wishing Stone Love Charm

In the Season of Hope you strike out towards your dreams, wishing they would come true. A wishing stone is an object that can contain all of your wishes and those of the person you love, the little ones and the big ones, holding them together in one symbolic place.

As a love charm, a wishing stone reminds you of the wishes you share with another and that you have remembered them. By using a wishing stone as a talisman to hold your wishes, you are taking the first step towards bringing them into reality. When you present the love charm, tell the person you love about the wishes it holds and invite him or her to fill it with their wishes, too. Listen to your partner's wishes. Perhaps each of you can fill the stone with new wishes as they come to you. Whenever you see the stone, remember each one of the wishes it contains, and think about how you might make one of them come true.

LEFT: *The wishing stone is an ancient charm for making your dreams come true. Often a person would make a wish as he dropped the stone into the sea or a wishing well.*

You will need

- Stone
- Pen and paper
- Paintbrush
- Coloured enamel paint
- Re-usable adhesive

1 Find a stone that you feel would make a good object to remember wishes by. Think about what the stone is made of, its shape and what marks and texture it has. Think of three wishes you have, wishes you would like to share with a special person. Try and imagine some patterns or shapes that remind you of those thoughts. Sketch them on paper. Keep the symbols of your wishes simple and bold; perhaps the outline of shapes or animals.

2 Paint the pattern on to the stone using enamel paints in colours you feel that the person you love would appreciate. Think of other patterns that you feel the person you are giving this to would like to see. Try and paint the stone all over its surface using all the colours. When you have finished painting, or if you need to pause during the painting, place the stone on a piece of re-usable adhesive to hold it upright.

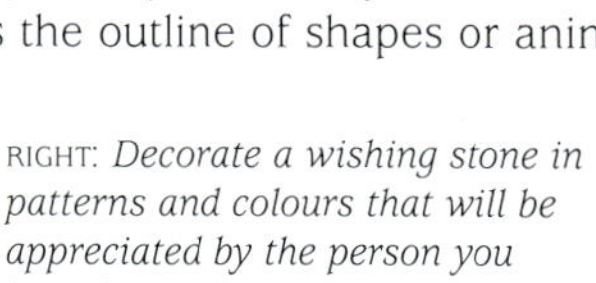

RIGHT: *Decorate a wishing stone in patterns and colours that will be appreciated by the person you love, for whom the stone is a gift.*

Season of Passion

When you can see and hear the other person for who he or she is, when you are completely open with him or her and it is reciprocal, then you are in a safe place to express the passion that fills your heart. This is the season of heat, of dance, of rapture and cries of joy. This is the season where you can leap into your dreams wholeheartedly, where you can reap the benefits of sharing and listening. Now you know the other person and know that your hearts beat to the same rhythm.

This is the season when two people move as one, when your passion for life spills over. Passion and love can be forces of tremendous change and it often takes courage to ride this season to its peak. Never be afraid to express your feelings, or embrace the other person's feelings with joy. When there are moments of disharmony, always remember the hopes you shared before, and remember how to listen and not to judge. At this time, if it is appropriate, you may decide to follow the heat of passion in lovemaking. This is a period when you give with every part of your being, without any regrets, guilt or mindless disrespect, but with honour and beauty.

In this time of rising passion, you lay your soul bare to the other person. You find the courage to show your vulnerability because this is the only way to share your deepest self with him or her. Sometimes when you feel vulnerable, you can put up defences, as the ego reluctantly relinquishes control of the heart and your past wounds, if still healing, are revealed. With these defences there is often irrational anger, a closing down and withdrawal of the person. You must always respect someone when you walk close to painful places. Let him or her be angry and offer understanding. Love understands grief, as it is part of the natural cycle.

In this season you must be mindful of the joy and the pain in the places where you light the fires of passion.

LEFT: *In the Season of Passion, as with nature flowering in summer, you become gloriously alive, your love can grow and you express your love with every fibre of your being.*

OPPOSITE: *Now is the time to open your heart and release your passion.*

Preparation

With passion comes expression. You must let your body, the truest expression of your soul, easily demonstrate your feelings. Try to become used to expressing yourself openly, in words and deeds. Be confident in your feelings, no one else may judge them. They are not right or wrong. Let your body language become more expressive.

Dance to some music you enjoy and feel comfortable moving your body. Experiment with moving different parts of it. Start by dancing with the head and neck, then with the shoulders. Bring in your arms, elbows, wrists and fingertips so that your whole upper body is in motion. Then introduce the movement of the spine, the sway of your hips, the thousand ways to move your legs and feet, even your toes. If you cannot move some parts of your body, move as much as you are able to. Do not be self-conscious. Just let your whole body express your feelings with the music. Dance for no one but yourself, just becoming comfortable with every pore of your body speaking your heart.

When you are with others be conscious of their physical presence; can you sense what they need? Would they benefit from a hug or a touch of hands? If you find it difficult to sense intuitively what might be appropriate, then do not be afraid to ask. Touch is one of the most important gifts we have to offer, by touching someone we remind them that they belong; that they are wanted and loved in this world. Be aware of your own needs, too. Speak up when you want a hug or even a massage. By asking for physical attention, you open the door for others to open up their hearts and express their love in a physical way.

Spend some time remembering the feeling of the person you love, retrace his or her skin in your mind. If you want to, spend some time together, both of you with your eyes closed. Run your fingers over each other, tracing the outline and contours of your faces. Then, when you are apart, see if you can recall the contours of their body.

LEFT: *Dancing encourages freedom of expression.*

ABOVE RIGHT: *Hugging your partner helps to bond a relationship.*

Meditation

This meditation is to aid relaxation and is designed to remind you of the sensation of your own body. Everyone is unique and you should take pleasure from this difference and offer it with joy. Play some relaxing music while performing this meditation to feel the full benefit.

1 Lie down on the floor, with something soft, such as a blanket or rug, beneath your back. Lie relaxed with your hands by your sides. Close your eyes, concentrate and try to feel your body. Notice which parts feel slightly tense and which feel completely relaxed.

2 Start with your toes. Breathing in, clench them up as hard as you can and then as you breathe out, release them. Next, do the same with your ankles. As you breathe in, tense them to bring your feet off the floor, and then relax as you breathe out.

3 Work your way slowly up your body, clenching and relaxing your knees, your thighs, your bottom, your stomach, your fingers and your shoulders, all the way up to your head. Finally, try to clench the scalp of your head and then relax it. Take a long, slow breath and relax. Notice your body again. If there are parts which still feel a little tense, repeat the exercise with them.

As you grow more proficient, you will be able to relax parts of your body more easily. This exercise also heightens the awareness of the body, helping you to feel it more intimately.

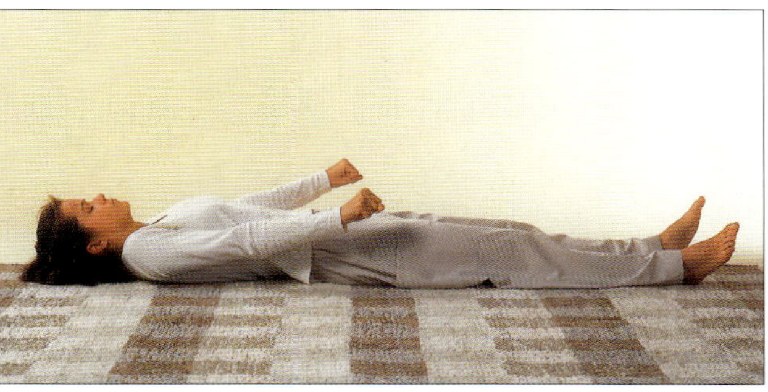

Garland Love Charm

Flowers and garlands have been used by many cultures to signify the eternal bond between two people, a circle that unites them. A garland of flowers and berries is especially significant, as both are signs of passion and fertility.

Think about which flowers and berries are in season and which you would like to weave into a garland. This garland can also be made into a crown.

It was customary for lovers to leave a garland on the door of their beloved on the first day of summer. Couples used to wear crowns of flowers on their marriage day, and it is still traditional for a bride today to wear some kind of floral headdress. The garland could also be a necklace or used as a decorative wall hanging.

When you give your love charm, tell the person you love how you feel about the bond that you share and what this garland means to you.

You will need

- Branches of leaves
- Flowers
- Ferns or other foliage
- Garden wire
- Garden string or wool (yarn)

LEFT: *The giving of a garland of flowers is an ancient summer custom throughout the world. The garland is a symbol of fertility and of the joining of two people into a single, unbroken, eternal circle of life.*

1 Collect branches of leaves and flowers, but always thank the tree or plant that gave you its fruit. You may also want to collect some berries, ferns or other foliage for the garland. Pull the length of garden wire into a circle and wrap the ends together to secure it. Take a branch and weave it around the circle. If it is not very flexible tie it into shape using the string or wool (yarn).

2 Moving around the circle, weave the branches around, and secure them where necessary with the string. Use the longer, greener branches first and then add the smaller flowers and plants. As you fold a new flower into the garland, think about what it signifies to you and what you would like the garland to bring to the person you are making it for.

3 Repeat this process until you have used up all your foliage and flowers and you are happy with the garland. Present it to the one you love and explain all the thoughts and feelings you have woven into its branches.

Eternity Band Love Charm

As a symbol of the bond that you share with a person, you can present him or her with an eternity band. This is a wristband that is tied on and, if possible, never removed until it wears through. It is made as a single circle and then cut in half; each person then wears one half of the band, signifying how the two people are one in their hearts. This is a very potent sign and you should think carefully whether it is the right time for you to share this with someone.

When you present this charm to someone you love, you may want to do so with some ceremony, for example during a meal, in the atmosphere of a lighted candle or in a special place. Tell your lover your feelings and your passions as you present the charm and explain what this eternity band signifies to you. If he accepts the gift, cut the band in half between knots using scissors. Each of you can then tie the other person's band into place and, if it feels right, seal the final knot with a kiss.

You will need

- Beads, shells, any other items
- Leather thong or lace

1 Begin by spending some time quietly, preparing your thoughts and capturing the intent with which you wish to fill the eternity band. Gather up small beads and shells and any other charms that you feel should be a part of the band.

2 Cut the length of thong or lace so that you can wrap it roughly three times around your wrist. Leave about 2 cm (¾ in) and tie a knot at one end of the thong. Think about the pattern that you want to make.

3 Begin threading on the beads and charms. Group the beads together by tying a knot in the thong or lace, then thread on the beads. Tie another knot to secure them into the pattern. Do this at frequent intervals.

4 When you have 2.5–5 cm (1–2 in) left, tie the last knot to secure the charms, then tie the two ends together.

5 Present the charm to your partner, cut the wristband in half and tie one half around one another's wrists.

Season of Fulfilment

Once passion has risen, peaked and found its natural balance, you will find there is a huge and wonderful space created between the person you love and yourself. It is a space where you are nurtured and where possibilities exist you had not even dreamed of before.

This is a time when you can reflect on your journey. You have the time to learn from all those mistakes in the past seasons. You may realize that you have reached a place which was not part of your dream and in which you must now find peace.

LEFT: *In the Season of Fulfilment, as in autumn, some things wither and die to make way for new growth.*

The Season of Fulfilment is associated with autumn. In the time after passion you become fulfilled and find calmness in your life. It is here that the true healing of love occurs. This can be a painful process as love discovers the deeper aspects of your heart and the healing of old wounds occurs.

Now you must also accept that this contentment is transitory. It will not last and should not last. If you are content for too long, you forget your dreams and stop the cycle of love from carrying on. If you get stuck here, if the cycle stops, so too will love and you may wake up one day and find it has left you completely.

In the time of fulfilment you are rejoicing in the journey so far, but also preparing for new dreams and letting go of old ones which you find you no longer yearn for.

It is a time of acceptance, honesty and the knowledge that all things change and that some things must perish for others to live.

The highest love of all finds its fulfilment not in what it keeps, but in what it gives.
Father Andrew SDC

Preparation

This is the season for looking at yourself carefully in the mirror, noticing the changes that have happened and accepting who you are and where you are.

Spend time alone thinking about what your dreams and hopes were at the beginning of the cycle, the time when you were last dreaming about who you are and what you want to do and be. Think about whether you have fulfilled those dreams or whether they still have meaning for you. Write down those dreams that no longer represent what you desire. Now think about yourself and how you have changed. Are there things that you don't like about yourself? What things are you glad to have gained from love? Write down all the things that you feel you have lost. As you write down each one, try to remember one thing you have gained that replaces it.

Think about and value the self-knowledge that you will inevitably acquire during the cycle. By opening your heart to another, you have looked deeper into yourself.

Finally, take a long look at your habits. Are you fixed in your ways? Are there habits that prevent you from accepting new aspects of your relationship? Write down all those habits and consciously make an effort to let go of them, and with each one think of a possibility that may open up by doing things differently.

Take all those words and put them to rest. Either build a fire for them, or bury them, or throw them into the sea or a lake. As you do so, remember all the wonderful gifts that the relationship has brought you.

LEFT: *As you reflect on the past cycle, make a note of your reassessment.*

Meditation

As you reach a time of change, you often find you become tense and full of dark thoughts as you resist the need to change. You often become angry, not wanting to let the cycle move on, but preferring to keep the status quo. This is a meditation for releasing any dark clouds of anger or frustration and replacing them with warmth and light, so that you are ready to accept whatever is ahead. It is especially good if practised first thing in the morning.

1 Stand with your feet shoulder-width apart and parallel. Keep your back straight, head up and your arms relaxed in front of you. Bend your knees slightly and close your eyes. Feel heavy in your body, sink your weight downwards so that you are firmly connected with the ground.

2 Bring your arms up in a wide circle and breathe in slowly and deeply through your nose. As you do so, imagine that the air you breathe in is full of white light, happiness and all the bright possibilities that the day holds before you.

3 Turn your palms downwards and bring your arms down in front of you, breathing out through your mouth. As you do so, imagine the air you are expelling is grey and dark, full of all the worries and frustrations of the past day or moments before. Let your hands come to rest at your sides again and repeat the exercise twice more.

Protective Love Charm

In many cultures giving a cloak or scarf signifies the offer of protection, that the person giving will be responsible for the wellbeing of the other.

You can give a decorated piece of fabric that symbolizes a cloak as a love charm to signify that you will always respect the other person. You are there should he need you, but equally you will remain folded away if he needs to be alone.

The size of the fabric can be large enough for physical warmth – perhaps you could find a real jacket to decorate – or it can be as small as a token handkerchief or scarf as it is here. A cloak has a deep connection with the blankets you were wrapped in as a baby: they offered peace to the heart. You can remind someone through touching the cloak or fabric token that you are always there when you are needed.

Think about the pattern or decorations to use on the fabric. For example, do you want an emblem signifying your love in the centre of the piece, or do you want to decorate only the borders? When you have finished preparing the fabric give it to the person you love as a folded parcel. Let him unfold it and place it around his shoulders, or accept it as a token of your intentions. Explain to him what your thoughts were while making it and what your feelings are now.

You will need

Square of fabric
Soft pencil
Needle and thread
Small pieces of fabric, beads and charms
Paintbrush
Fabric paints or embroidery thread (floss)

LEFT: *Giving a protective love charm symbolizes the intention to respect your partner through life.*

1 Select the material and colour carefully, imagining what will feel the most warming to the recipient.

2 Draw out the pattern on the cloth, using a pencil. Think about the images and symbols.

3 Sew on the pieces of fabric you have chosen. You can also tie on beads and other charms if you feel they are needed.

4 Now use either fabric paints or embroidery thread (floss) to fill in the pattern.

Talking Stick Love Charm

The talking stick is a Native American charm to help people communicate during difficult times. It can be made of any material, although traditionally it was a carved wooden stick.

A talking stick love charm can be made for any unspoken problem. Use it as a way of moving forward in a relationship, accepting changes as they are encountered. To use a talking stick, place it in front of both of you. If one of you wishes to speak, you can then pick up the stick. The other person must listen intently and respectfully in silence. When the speaker has finished he or she replaces the stick on the ground for the other person to pick up and speak. Here, for this Season of Fulfilment and healing, the stick is made as a rolled scroll of paper.

Consider what inscription you would like to put on the scroll. This will be hidden during the time you are talking and, after you have both said what it is that you need to, the scroll or talking stick can be burnt to symbolize that the issue is now forgotten.

You will need

- Coloured paints or pencils
- Paintbrush
- Paper or cardboard
- Coloured ribbon or wool (yarn)

LEFT: *Burning the talking stick signifies that the problem has been discussed, released and can be forgotten.*

1 Using the coloured pencils or paints, draw out the inscription on the paper. Spend time designing and choosing the words or symbols, remembering that they indicate talking and listening to the person you love.

2 Paint on the design and let it dry. As you paint each brushstroke, think about listening to the person you love, and about letting go of the problem so that you can both live without its shadow over you.

3 Roll up the paper into a scroll, and secure it with some wool (yarn) or ribbon. The symbols along with your intentions are now bound with the roll of the charm.

4 Present the charm to the person you love and suggest how it may be used. If you both feel the need to talk about something that is difficult, use it as described, so that one listens while the other speaks, holding the stick. When you both feel you have finished, throw the talking stick on to a fire and watch the flames devour it, symbolizing the healing and end to the issue.

Final Word

Love is a gift that we all share, as friends, as family, as all creatures living together on this wonderful Earth. At every moment we are given a chance to express that connection, whether it be hugging a friend or offering what we have to those who go without.

To love someone is a truly precious and joyous feeling, but it is also one that will constantly challenge you to listen to and learn from. Love is a living thing. When you stop listening and give up learning then the beauty of it withers and fades.

Love charms are gifts, tools and special places where you can remind yourself of the beauty that you share with someone, or reawaken something that has shrivelled up from neglect. They can help turn your dreams into a reality and take you on in the cycle to create more dreams and more special moments in your life.

It sometimes takes courage and determination to follow the cycle of love. You must always be listening to the voice of your heart so that you can move ever forwards towards your dream. There may be times when you must weep for what you have lost, but there will be other times when you will cry out with joy at what you have gained. Everyone walks the cycle of love, and its changing seasons carry them onwards to happiness and the life of their dreams.

Love charming is an art that everyone possesses; they are born with its knowledge beating inside them. You can practise this art of bringing love to everyone around you as part of the everyday world. In so doing, you become the warm, loving person that you truly are at heart.

May you walk a path of beauty and love every moment of your life and so live the life of your dreams.

LEFT: *The lovers,* Paolo and Francesca da Rimini, *1867 by Dante Gabriel Rossetti (1828–1882).*

OPPOSITE: Venus Verticordia, *1864–68 by Dante Gabriel Rossetti.*

Rune	Letter	Name	Table of Rune Symbols for Love Charms
ᚠ	F	Feoh	Wealth, riches and blessings for a new beginning
ᚢ	U	Ur	The strength and perseverance of the wild ox
ᚦ	Th	Thorn	Protection of thorns around the heart
ᚨ	A	Ansuz	Speaking and telling of charms and dreams
ᚱ	R	Rad	Turning the wheel and cycle of love
ᚲ	K	Ken	Bringing the light of understanding and acceptance
ᚷ	G	Gyfu	The giving and sharing of equals
ᚹ	W	Wyn	Joy of life when you are walking the path to your dreams
ᚺ	H	Hagal	Destruction of the old and letting go of the past
ᚾ	N	Nyd	The need for love, which burns in your heart
ᛁ	I	Is	Sudden endings, frozen and broken in a moment
ᛃ	J	Jera	Celebrating the seasons of love
ᛇ	Z	Eihwaz	Eternity of love and its cycle of creation, death and renewal
ᛈ	P	Peorth	The freedom of choice to make your own choices
ᛉ	X	Elhaz	Protection and resistance against ill-intended actions
ᛊ	S	Sigel	The sun at dawn, bringing light to the dark places in your life
ᛏ	T	Tiwaz	Justice and truth everywhere beneath the spinning sky
ᛒ	B	Beorc	The birth of fertile new beginnings
ᛖ	E	Ehwaz	The loyalty and faithfulness of the horse
ᛗ	M	Man	Connection of each person as human beings on Earth
ᛚ	L	Lagu	Water to help your life and love grow
ᛜ	Ng	Ing	Spreading the boundless light of your heart out into the world
ᛟ	O	Odal	Creating a space in your life which you can call your own
ᛞ	D	Dag	Welcoming in bright intentions and warding off dark ones

Tree	Letter	Old Name	Table of Trees for Love Charms
Birch	B	Beth	Sweep away the dark places in your heart to allow something new to grow
Rowan	L	Luis	The protection of fire against the dark
Ash	N	Nion	Force of creation allowing you to form reality from your dreams
Alder	F	Fearn	Emotional strength and perseverance
Willow	S	Saille	Flowing, cleansing water of healing
Hawthorn	H	Huath	Birth of possibilities and hope
Oak	D	Duir	Doorway through to understanding of the heart
Holly	T	Tinne	Never-ending watchfulness
Hazel	C	Coll	Listening to your dreams and taking the initiative to make them happen
Bramble	M	Muin	Bringing about change in your life and dreams
Ivy	G	Gort	Determination and strength in walking around the cycle of love
Reed	Ng	Ngetal	Speaking and writing words from your heart
Elder	R	Ruis	Calling the magic of love into your life
Apple	Q	Quert	Sharing the limitless love in the world
Blackthorn	St	Straif	Projection of your heart and feelings out into the world
Elm	A	Ailm	Growing onwards and upwards to rise above the difficulties in life
Gorse	O	Onn	Hope of what love will bring
Heather	U	Ur	Renewing and refreshing old or tired love
Poplar	E	Eadha	Directing your feelings towards a particular person or place in your life
Yew	I	Iubhar	Learning from the past and letting it go

MOON WISDOM

For millennia the moon has featured in mythology across the world. Ancient civilizations venerated the moon for her self-regenerative ability in waxing and waning, and for her influence over the germination and growth of crops. In modern times we can learn how to harness the moon's powers as she moves through her phases and cycles.

The Nature of the Moon

The moon is powerful and mysterious, influencing not only the tides and the weather, but also our moods and behaviour. She is also strongly associated with the imagination and with psychic, intuitive powers.

The moon is known by many names and is worshipped by many cultures throughout the world. Many ancient civilizations venerated the moon because they saw how she influenced the germination and growth of crops. She was revered for her self-regenerative ability in waxing and waning. Even the dark time of the moon was seen to hold secrets about death and the veil that separates spirit from matter. Her ancient worshippers knew her as the "Queen of Heaven", believing she held the key to the rhythms and cycles of existence and of the natural world.

The moon inspires wonder when we see her fullness in the sky, shining her silver light upon the shadows of the night. Both men and women are intimately linked to her changing faces of crescent, full, waning and dark, as she progresses through her lunar cycle. When she pulls and tugs at the waters of the earth, creating high and low tides, she also pulls at the water within our bodies, affecting our moods, our sleep patterns, health and women's moontime cycles. It has been well documented that the full moon has a powerful effect upon our mental and emotional stability.

Because the moon is well within the gravitational field of the earth, interaction with us and her elliptical orbit affects weather patterns. Tropical storms, tidal waves, hurricanes, earthquakes and heavy rainfall have all been associated with lunar activity. This section will take you on a journey to meet Mother Moon and will help you to understand the nature of her rhythms and cycles. May your spirit meet with her and may the secrets of the moon be revealed to you.

SALLY MORNINGSTAR

LEFT AND OPPOSITE: *Because of the interaction of moon and earth, the moon is linked to fertility and childbirth. There are more births at the full moon than at any other time in the lunar cycle, and for thousands of years moon deities have been called upon to increase fertility and aid conception.*

ABOVE: *Moon festivals of ancient times were often celebrated with music and dance. Music has long been associated with the moon. The sacred dances would climax in orgiastic rites or sacrifices, to ensure good crop yields, fair weather and health for the tribal community.*

Lunar Superstitions

- ☆ As the bringer of new opportunity, the new moon marks an auspicious time to turn coins in your pocket while bowing to the crescent in the night sky, to encourage your finances to grow.
- ☆ You should not leave your washing out at night. If moonlight shines upon it, it shines upon clothes for a funeral.
- ☆ If you touch a silver coin when you see the moon, it will bring good luck.
- ☆ Move house on a new moon.
- ☆ It is considered very unlucky to marry during the month of May or during any of the waning/dark quarters. Conversely, it is considered lucky to marry in June and during any waxing or full moon phase, but do not let the light of the moon shine upon your nuptial bed, or you will court bad luck.
- ☆ A baby born at the time of a full moon is a child of fortune.
- ☆ It is lucky to hold a newborn child up to the light of a new moon, and give thanks as well as prayers for a long life.

supporting and nurturing life on earth. The spider is universally linked to the life-giving qualities of the moon.

The snail, because of its moisture trail and its seeming ability to vanish and reappear, is also linked to the moon. It was thought that the snail could travel into the underworld and re-emerge unharmed. The Mexican moon god, Tecciztecatl, was depicted in the shell of a snail.

Mirrors figure prominently in moon lore, because of their reflective qualities, and have long been used for divination purposes. In Britain, in the 19th century, it was a common folk custom for girls and young women to use a mirror and the full moon to see how long it would be before they were married. Two and a half thousand years earlier, it is said that Pythagoras was taught mirror divination by the wise women of Thessaly.

LEFT: *The unicorn represents the lunar power in mythology as the lion does the sun. In heraldry, the two pictured together draw upon the complementary powers of the sun and the moon.*

Moon Goddesses

Many ancient civilizations venerated the moon because they saw how she influenced the germination and growth of crops, how she matched the average female menstrual cycle of 28–30 days, and how she affected weather, as well as her self-regenerative ability in waxing and waning – appearing and then disappearing again. Even the dark time of the moon was seen to hold secrets about death and the veil that separates spirit from matter. Her ancient worshippers knew her as the "Queen of Heaven", and could see that she held the key to a deep and profound wisdom about the rhythms and cycles of human existence and the natural world.

ABOVE: *The moon goddess, Venus*

ABOVE: *A triform statue of Hecate*

In order to find ways to express their beliefs, at a time when the structure of the cosmos was still a mystery, they turned to archetypes that personified these beliefs in the form of gods and goddesses. Because it was important to differentiate between the phases of the moon, different goddesses represented each phase – a privilege not given to any other heavenly presence. The Greeks, for example, worshipped Artemis as the new moon, Selene as the full moon and Hecate as the waning and dark moon. All the goddesses from across the ages are really one and the same, blending and moving together to weave the powers of the moon into immortal form.

Goddesses of the moon were absorbed into other cultures as civilizations evolved. The Greek Artemis became Diana in Rome, for example, and Ma'at, goddess of truth and the consort of the Egyptian moon god Thoth, was known by the Gnostics as Sophia. The cult of the Egyptian goddess Isis, the "Good Mother", spread throughout Greece and the Roman Empire and lasted well into the Christian era, to be eventually absorbed

RIGHT: *The moon goddess Selene pictured here with Endymion by Poussin*

ABOVE: *Diana was a Roman triple goddess – the virgin, the mother of nature, and the huntress. As huntress she is the destroyer aspect of the moon.*

by the cult of the Virgin Mary, who was also a lady of the moon. So strong was the compulsion to honour the moon goddess and keep her favour, that sacrifices and rites were performed in the hope that by appeasing her, she would be sympathetic to the very basic human needs for food, water and regeneration.

All phases of the moon held secrets about the circle of life. By worshipping the appropriate moon goddess, human beings could relate to (and try to tame) her influence.

Goddesses of the Moon

The moon goddess is also called the "Triple Goddess" because of her three phases, new, full and waning/dark. The Triple Goddess represents the maiden, the mother and the crone and is also known as the "Great Mother" or "Magna Dei". There are also gods of the moon, and one of these is the Egyptian god Thoth, while another is the Sumerian god Sin.

***Artemis,* Greek,** carrying a quiver filled with arrows and a bow, accompanied by lionesses, deer and birds: childbirth.

***Selene,* Greek,** wearing wings and a headband, riding in a chariot drawn by white horses: magic.

***Diana,* Roman,** carrying a bow and arrow, with a hound and stag: fertility and nature.

***Hecate,* Greek,** a goddess who has three heads, usually standing back-to-back with a horse, hound and lioness: magic, sorcery, death and the underworld.

Sophia of Phrygia, female representation of the holy spirit: divine knowledge and wisdom.

***Arianrhod,* Celtic,** wearing silver robes and holding a silver wheel: divination.

***Ceridwen,* Celtic** dark moon goddess, with a cauldron, and a white sow: herbs and grains, divination, spells, death.

***Isis (above,* Egyptian,** wearing a crescent headdress supporting a full moon: magic, fertility, regeneration.

***Cybele,* Phrygian,** the dark moon goddess, wearing a crescent moon headdress, with pomegranates and bees, carrying finger bones: nature, wild beasts and dark magic.

The Angel of the Moon

As the Great Mother, the moon has considerable influence over her human "children", as do angels. The angel associated with the moon is Gabriel, the healer. Gabriel is usually referred to as "he", although in fact angels are neither male nor female. He is the Angel of the Annunciation, who visited the Virgin Mary (who is a lady of the moon), and his visit is described in a hymn: "The Angel Gabriel from Heaven came, his wings as drifted snow, his eyes as flame". He is sometimes depicted carrying white lilies, the flowers of the Virgin, and is intimately linked with healing and alleviating suffering.

On the lunar wheel Gabriel stands in the west, in the position of the waning moon. The direction of west is represented by the water element. If you are seeking healing, or performing healing ceremonies for others, stand facing the west during the time of a waning moon to say prayers for healing. You should also face west in order to make a water offering.

A water offering can be anything that is taken from the waters of the earth, such as watercress, a river stone, seaweed or a shell. You may wish to seek out a scallop or other large shell and fill it with spring water for any healing ceremonies that you are performing.

ABOVE : *Gabriel is often depicted carrying white lilies.*

RIGHT: *The power of Gabriel's spiritual flames can charge any environment that he enters. He has dominion over all diseases and so has great healing powers.*

An Angel Healing

Perform this ceremony just after a full moon to seek healing for someone who is sick. Choose camphor, eucalyptus or sandalwood as your fragrant aroma. All these fragrances are linked to the healing qualities of the moon.

You Will Need

- 2 light blue candles
- crystal
- white lilies
- water offering
- aromatherapy burner
- matches
- 9 drops of eucalyptus, sandalwood or camphor oil
- 9 white nightlights
- pen with silver ink
- natural paper
- heatproof container

1 Put the two blue candles in the centre of a table with the crystal, flowers, water offering and the burner. Light the candles and burner. Fill the burner with water and add the oil.

2 Place the nightlights in a circle around the other items and light them all.

3 Write the name of the person to be healed, and their ailment, on a piece of paper. Fold it twice and hold it in your hands, saying, "Angel Gabriel I ask for your help. Please bring your healing touch to [name]. By divine will, remove [this condition] from [name], for the highest good of all."

4 Take the piece of paper, light it in the flame of a candle, then drop it heatproof bowl, while visualizing the ailment being lifted out of the person and carried away by Gabriel. Give thanks for the healing vibrations, blow out all the candles and close the healing by putting the nightlights away.

Animal Totems of the Moon

Certain animals have long and deep links with the moon and have become her totems. In addition to these, any animal linked to moisture, seas, rivers, and lakes will be pertinent to the moon.

Wolf

The wolf has been linked with the psychic aspects of lunar lore and with baying during the full moon. Legends about people turning into werewolves at a full moon may be based upon a certain amount of fact. The symptoms of a rare medical condition called lycanthropy, in which a patient has fantasies of being a wolf, seem to be triggered by the full moon, and this could be the basis of werewolf legends.

LEFT: *The wolf is strongly linked with psychic aspects of the moon.*

Hare

Pictorial images of the hare have been found in Assyrian reliefs and in ancient Egypt paintings and carvings. The myth of the "hare in the moon" is well known in the Far East, Africa, South America and Europe. The hare represents the lunar cycles: from new to full and waning to dark; from conception to gestation; and from growth to decline and death. Long associated with fertility and the fertility cycle, the hare was considered to be androgynous (having both male and female attributes). This was representative of the way they perceived the moon: the waxing moon was the male aspect, and the waning moon was the female aspect.

The Anglo-Saxon goddess of fertility, Eostre, was depicted with the head of a hare, and in many cultures – Celtic, Indian, Buddhist, Chinese, and Native American – deities of the moon were illustrated carrying a hare. The Native American hero Manabazho, portrayed as a hare, is an important symbol of creation.

Seek hare medicine when performing fertility rites, prayers or wishes, when seeking joy and illumination, or when you need quick and effective results.

ABOVE: *The hare is linked to the spring festival of Eostre and is a symbol of the birth of new life and the beginning of a fertile cycle.*

Frog

The frog is the bringer of the rains, as well as a fertility symbol associated with the moon. Hekt, the frog goddess of the ancient Egyptians, carried the potential of the fertile waters that symbolize birth and fertility, and the green frog found in the Nile region was venerated as the bringer of new life.

The frog is also a totem clan animal of the Native Americans, for whom it is a symbol of the water element, a powerful cleanser. The sacred Manitou ("Great Spirit") of the Algonquin people lives in the moon and influences the waters of the world, as well as the weather. Weather, like anything associated with water, has a connection with the moon, because of her strong influence upon it.

Seek frog medicine when you want to move from one situation to another without obstacles, when working on cleansing the emotions, and during any fertility prayers.

ABOVE: *It was long thought that the souls of the dead were carried by frogs to the moon. Frog talismans, which have been discovered in ancient Egyptian tombs, are likely to have been symbols of resurrection into the spirit world of the moon.*

Cat

The cat is an animal that is difficult to get to know, and which maintains a certain distance and mystery. It is associated with the Greek goddess Artemis, known in Roman mythology as Diana. Bast,a cat-headed goddess, was worshipped by the ancient Egyptians; they were held in such high esteem that to hurt or destroy a cat in Egypt was punishable by death.

The cat has long been known as a "familiar" to magical practitioners, especially those working with lunar magic. In other cultures, too, the mythology of the cat can be seen as important. For example, Shosti, the Hindu goddess of childbirth, is depicted riding a cat, and Freya, the Norse goddess of love and fertility, is shown riding in a cat-drawn carriage. As a symbol of the moon, the cat represents mystery. In Christian medieval Europe the black cat was relegated to the realms of witchcraft and sorcery rather than being seen as a representative of the moon's teachings.

Seek cat medicine when you want to improve your psychic abilities, or perhaps when performing a psychic protection ceremony. Call on the Egyptian goddess Bast when looking for a lost cat, as she has great influence with feline creatures.

ABOVE: *Part of human domestic life but also leading an independent life of mystery, particularly at night, the cat's affinity to the moon is profound.*

LEFT: *The cow is also associated with the moon, because her horns look like the crescent or new moon.*

Owl

Owls represent wisdom and are commonly heard at night during the full moon in the winter months, remaining silent for most of the rest of the year. Linked to Hecate, goddess of the dark moon, the appearance of an owl is sometimes associated with the subsequent death of someone close. Rather than being of evil intent, the sound of the owl's call, or the sudden or unusual appearance of one, should be seen as reassurance that the spirit of the moon is calling to help the soul back to its true home.

The owl can also represent deep fears, the unconscious, and fear of the dark. Hearing an owl close by may not signify a death, but rather a call to understand something about yourself that resides deep within your psyche. Seek the wisdom of owl medicine when you are in a spiritual or life-changing crisis.

Cow

Sacred animal of Isis, the mother goddess of ancient Egypt, the cow represents fertility. She is also the giver of milk that nourishes human life, as well as the life of her calf. Milk, like water, is associated with the gifts of the moon. The moon goddess was worshipped in ancient Egypt as a golden, long-horned cow. At the winter solstice, Isis, crowned as the moon-cow, would circle the coffin of her consort, Osiris, seven times. This symbolized the seven circlings of the moon from winter to summer, signifying the turning of the wheel to new life and the resurrection of the universal spirit.

People of the buffalo clan, in Native American traditions, are the prayer weavers; seek bovine medicine or the assistance of the sacred cow, or use items symbolizing the cow, when saying prayers or seeking spiritual illumination.

ABOVE: *The owl is a harbinger of death and is associated with Hecate, the goddess of the dark moon.*

Other Animal Totems

Other animals associated with the moon are the toad, the lion, the bear and the fox. In Chinese mythology, a three-legged toad represents the yin, or female, aspect of life, and the traditional explanation for a lunar eclipse was that the toad had swallowed the moon. Some Native American tribes associate the toad with the dark phase of the moon's cycle – in other words, the deeper, more silent time when wisdom can be taught and found.

ABOVE: *The lioness is sacred to the Phrygian goddess, Cybele.*

The lion has long represented the powers of the sun, but the lioness represents the powers of the moon and several cultures have depicted lionesses with lunar deities.

The bear is linked to the moon goddess Diana. As one of the great shamanic animals, said to be responsible for teaching the sacred medicine way, it is no surprise that the bear has come to be associated with the teachings of the moon's wisdom.

The fox, long known for his cunning and ability to shapeshift, is known in North America and Japan as the bringer of rain. As such, he has links with the atmospheric influences of the moon upon the weather.

Moon totem animals can be carried as charms or talismans, which should ideally be made of silver, the metal of the moon. Dreams about any of the moon totem animals could well signify that an important change is imminent, or may signify a time of increased fertility (such as ovulation), a birth, death of the old, or a time for learning and growth.

Animal Associations with the Triple Goddess

New moon: hare, cow, frog – Artemis, the maiden.

Full moon: bear, dove, hare, cow, cat, frog, wolf, stag – Diana, Isis, Selene, Arianrhod, the mother.

Waning and dark moon: owl, serpent, hound, bat, fox, toad – Hecate, Ceridwen, Cybele, the crone.

LEFT: *Isis wore a headdress that symbolized her virtues and associations. Her crown is a crescent moon supporting the full moon.*

BELOW: *In Celtic mythology, the bear was a lunar power, also associated with King Arthur.*

Moon Signs

In astrology, the position of the sun at birth represents your outer personality, whereas the position of the moon indicates your inner world of feelings and emotions. To discover the position of the moon at your birth, you will need to consult an astrologer for a natal chart. Once this has been established, you can refer to the information in the relevant section below.

Moon in Aries

Aries moon people tend to be impulsive and hasty, with a tendency to make quick (and sometimes rash) decisions. Their impulsiveness can make them impatient, and so increase the probability of accidents because of the speed at which they like to travel. They have quick and agile minds and are natural leaders, but need to guard against being bossy, overbearing, arrogant, or dismissive of others. If they learn how to harness this moon's powers, they can become excellent leaders, public speakers and pioneers.

Aries moons crave independence and can feel trapped by possessive or jealous behaviour. They do not understand the depths of emotions or feel particularly comfortable with them. As this is a fire moon, their feelings are very self-orientated. In fact, of all the faults that an Aries moon may have, selfishness is the greatest challenge to overcome. They are forward thinkers, inspired by new and challenging opportunities, wanting to carve their own path through life. People with their moon in Aries will be innovators in business, but need to learn to follow through anything they start. However, because of their "go it alone" attitude, Aries moons can sometimes be insensitive and thoughtless. Once a deeper understanding of this moon is reached, they will often regret things that they have said or done through lack of sensitivity and will then try to make up for it in some way.

ABOVE: *When the moon is transiting Aries, there will be an increase in fiery energy, leading to the potential for confrontations, but by remaining sensitive to others Aries moons can motivate without dominating. Arguments aside, this moontime is excellent for calling in the new and for taking steps towards a goal, bringing as it does an upsurge of willpower and determination.*

Stones
diamond, bloodstone

Flower
wild rose

Animal
ram

Moon in Taurus

People with their moon in Taurus are easy-going, relaxed and generally fun to be with. They appreciate fine art, music and the creative arts, as well as good food. Taurus moons are happy hosts, enjoying entertaining and providing entertainment to friends and family alike. These people are sensualists, with a love of beautiful things. They can, however, have a tendency to get stuck in ritual and routine. They dislike change and may be stubborn and inflexible, unless, of course, it is their own decision to change. They will not be pushed into anything.

Taurus moons are careful with money. Being materialistic, they like to buy good-quality products and will work hard to be able to afford them. This moon's message is that life is for enjoying, but they must guard against becoming addicted to rich and unhealthy foods. A healthy diet is vital for the Taurus moon, or the constitution will be weakened.

Taurus moons can feel very threatened by any challenges to their family life, and will do anything to maintain security. They are sensitive to the opinions of neighbours and the wider community, and are traditionalists. Their conformist attitudes can sometimes be stifling to those around them – a tendency to possessiveness is the greatest challenge they need to overcome.

Above all, Taurus moons are practical and down-to-earth. They provide a safe environment for children to grow up in, but need to allow their children to express their true personalities and not what is acceptable or expected of them. Letting the children go is the hardest lesson for Taurus moon parents.

ABOVE: *When the moon is passing through Taurus, be careful with your possessions, ensuring your home is secure if you need to go away. Take care of personal finances, and practical matters. When the new moon is in Taurus, it is a good time to begin longer term projects that may take a while to come to fruition.*

Moon in Gemini

People with their moon in Gemini are mentally agile, flitting from one idea to another with great ease. With this natural tendency, Gemini moons will have many projects on the go and need to learn to complete what they begin. Loose tongues need to be guarded against – Gemini moons can be gossips and chatterboxes, because of their love of the spoken word (and the sound of their own voices). The greatest challenges for Gemini moons are an appreciation of silence and the consolidation of actions.

Boredom sets in quickly with this placement, because their minds are constantly thinking up better ideas or solutions to problems. Their quick-wittedness and versatility is therefore a strength as well as a potential weakness. Once understanding of how to harness an agile mind into practical action is mastered, this sign is an asset in many situations. However, because of their tendency to move on quickly (unless the conversation is fascinating), they often miss opportunities to learn from, or understand, others.

Gemini moons find emotional people difficult to be around, and often have difficulty expressing their own feelings. They are drawn to the lighter side of life, where chatting and social interaction prevail. As long as they have stimulating outlets for their inspirations and sociability, they will be happy and content. They make excellent speakers, teachers, journalists and anything associated with the use of language. Gemini parents like to stimulate the minds of their children and provide opportunities to explore. They find it difficult to remain constant but are fun to be with and will spend hours with their family.

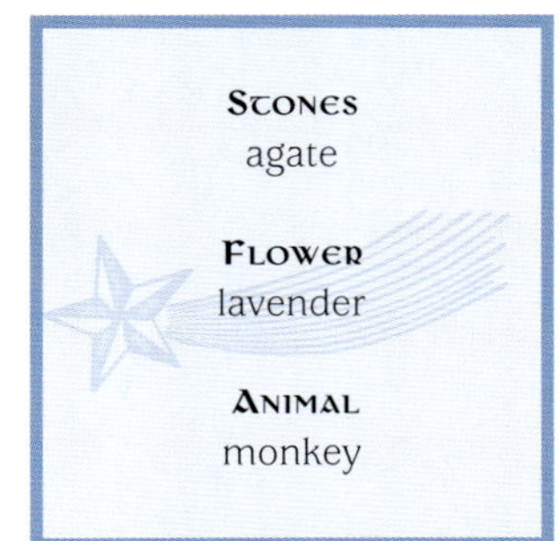

Stones
agate

Flower
lavender

Animal
monkey

ABOVE: *When the moon is transiting Gemini it is an important time to make sure that everything is based on fact, not to get carried away, and to guard against being too flippant about responsibilities. Be aware that stress will be an issue during this time, with an increase in the possibility of nervous tension and exhaustion.*

Moon in Cancer

The moon is exalted in Cancer. This means that she is in her best placement here. The moon governs this zodiacal sign and so will be a powerful influence in the chart when placed here. Cancer moon people are highly sensitive and crave emotional security. They need to be accepted for who they are, so can become extremely defensive when challenged. They are sensitive to atmospheres and are very intuitive. Their feelings are often correct, but they need to guard against presuming they are correct all the time, falling into the negative trap of feeling wronged, hurt or rejected. Learning how to accept the feelings and opinions of others will bring a great release to the anxieties that can be experienced by Cancer moons.

Cancer moon people are the carers of the zodiac, taking on the sick and weak in order to care for those less fortunate than themselves. This does not challenge their position and yet gives them the opportunity to excel in what they do best, but this caring should not be allowed to spill over into obsessional behaviour. They must learn to let others make their own mistakes and try not to rescue everyone they perceive is in need. They can be possessive and clingy in relationships, often retreating from areas of conflict instead of discussing them. They have a tendency towards self pity and sometimes have a moody and unpredictable side. They will not reveal anything until they are ready, and can over-exaggerate as their emotions take them on a roller-coaster of different realities and conclusions, often leading them to expect the worst. Cancer moon women can suffer more than most from pre-menstrual tension.

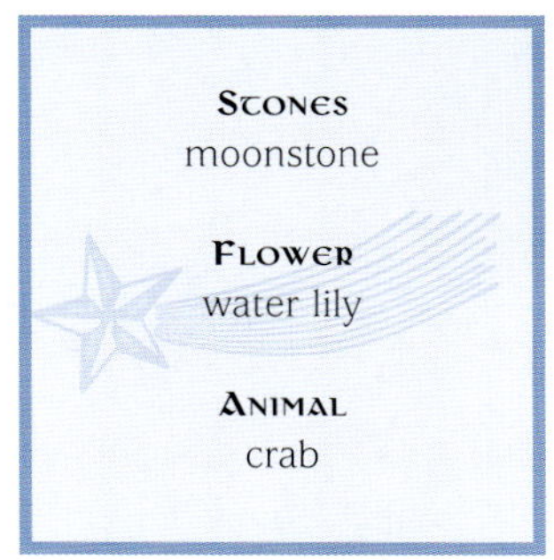

Stones
moonstone

Flower
water lily

Animal
crab

ABOVE: *Cancer moon people make ideal parents because of their desire to be needed, they are sensitive, caring and supportive of their children. When the moon is transiting Cancer, it is a good time to spend with the family, or help others. Try to avoid depressing situations, which will be prevalent during this time.*

MOON IN LEO

Moon in Leo people are naturally gregarious and love being the centre of attention. They know little fear and will have a go at most things, believing that everything is attainable. They may tend to be bossy and self-centred, believing, as they do, that they are the best at everything. This is a double-edged tendency, because they can also be great motivators to others who may lack their level of confidence. Leo moons love the limelight and may well be attracted to the creative arts, theatre, dance, or anything that allows them self-expression. They need to ensure that they find ways to balance their extrovert side with steadying activities that slow them down a little. They can bombard their way through life, completely unaware of their effect upon others, as they climb to the top.

Above all, Leo moons need to be recognized and appreciated. Like the lioness, Leo moon people are proud and able. They love romance and romantic interludes, and may often have a string of admirers who adore them. It is important to learn humility when your moon is in Leo and to sprinkle this over a naturally flamboyant lifestyle.

Caution is not the strongest characteristic when the moon is placed here. Think before you act, and plan before you begin, otherwise several very creative ideas may get lost in a whirl of self-aggrandizement.

Leo moons are sociable people and enjoy mixing with others. As parents, they see their children as extensions of their own egos, and so will push them to succeed. However, this pressure can be negative and can cause a child to leave home early if they find the levels of control or domination are just too overwhelming.

STONES
ruby

FLOWER
sunflower

ANIMAL
lion

ABOVE: *At a time when the moon is transiting Leo, electrical equipment can go wrong, so it is not a good time to shop for new gadgets or electrical appliances, especially if you are a Leo moon person. Guard against being self-centred, over-opinionated or pushy when in this astrological phase.*

Moon in Virgo

Moon in Virgo people are discriminating and exacting. They are extremely clean and tidy – meticulous, in fact. Everything has its place when the moon is in this sign. Virgo moons are tactful and diplomatic, so make excellent peacemakers and negotiators. They tend to be nervous and highly strung, lacking a basic confidence in their abilities. Their way with words can sometimes be wonderful, and writers often have their moon in this sign. They need to guard against being too critical or judgemental: their high standards and expectations can make others feel inadequate or uncomfortable. They are highly practical, and excel in most things they attempt, because they are methodical in their approach. Attention to detail means that their homes are spotless, their offices organized, and all plans are made with care, leaving little room for error. This strictness can be limiting sometimes, and learning a level of flexibility and fluidity can, therefore, be highly beneficial. Virgo moons are generally conscientious about their health, but need to guard against becoming fitness gurus to friends and family, because of their own obsessions with health.

Virgo moons are steady and reliable partners, good at handling and investing money. They approach parenting in the same way as everything else – with orderly correctness. The children are well turned out, their rooms are clean and tidy and everything is "taken care of" on a practical level. However, paranoia about mess can cause friction in the family, and Virgo moon parents need to learn how to loosen up and allow their children the freedom to loosen up and get themselves dirty once in a while.

Stones
jade

Flower
buttercup

Animal
cat

ABOVE: *When the moon is transiting Virgo, issues surrounding health and exercise will arise. This is a good time to begin a healthy eating plan or begin regular visits to the gym, as well as having a medical check-up. Keep things practical, and try not to be too critical and judgemental during this moon.*

Moon in Libra

ABOVE: *Moon in Libra people reside where there is harmony, creating lovely homes with relaxing environments for themselves and their families. When the moon is passing through Libra it is a good time to focus upon harmony within relationships, but not a time to make any serious decisions.*

Moon in Libra people love beauty and harmony. They are naturally charming and likeable, able to see many different points of view. This makes them excellent diplomats, lawyers or politicians. This ability, however, can also be a hindrance, leaving Libra moons uncertain and indecisive: decision-making is quite distasteful to them. They are understanding and sensitive to the thoughts and feelings of others, which means that they can often be used as a shoulder to cry on, or a place of refuge. However, other people would be wise to understand that the Libra moon's sensitivity can also be withdrawn if it is taken for granted or seen as a weakness.

Libra moons love beautiful things and the good things in life. Being naturally creative, their homes are artistically decorated and put together, even if little money is available. This artistic streak can also extend into their working lives with a job in the performing or visual arts, such as theatre, painting, dance or music.

They fall in love easily and enjoy their relationships, having a need to relate to other people. They must, however, avoid escapism and learn to face up to their own faults. Disharmony in the home can lead quite quickly to ill health, producing headaches and physical tension.

Libra parents want to share their cultured interests with their children, involving them in the arts in some form or other. This can lead to conflicts, if the children have no interest in such things. Libra moon parents need to allow their offspring to develop their own identity, follow their own particular talents and allow their creativity to shine however they choose.

Stones
opal

Flower
violet

Animal
hare

Moon in Scorpio

People with their moon in Scorpio will be intensely secretive and difficult to fathom, and any hurts will be stored away for a long, long time. Scorpio moons need to have the company of positive friends to help to lift them out of these depths into the fresh air of fun and laughter. The lighthearted side of life often escapes them, and they are sometimes much too serious, or even moody. This can lead to drug abuse or addictive patterns of behaviour. Scorpio moons need to learn how to channel their feelings into such things as self-healing, team games, and a healthy routine, instead of turning any negativity on to others or, even worse, upon themselves.

Scorpio moons can, however, utilize their intuitive skills in medicine, research, healing and detective work, and they are happiest when left to get on with a task quietly. Talented, because of their deep nature, Scorpio moons may end up in positions of power, but will be bosses that no one really understands. This is because Scorpio moons have difficulty with trust and openness. In relationships, they have a lot to give, if they will let go enough to give it. They should learn not to bear grudges or carry hurt feelings for too long, learning instead how to forgive and move on.

Scorpio moon parents are fiercely protective of their offspring, sometimes bordering on possessiveness with feelings of jealousy when other people are involved with their children – for example teachers, friends or grandparents. They need to understand that children need a diversity of relationships in order to develop a well-rounded sociability. Protectiveness is very supportive when necessary, but stifling when it is not.

Stones
topaz

Flower
chrysanthemum

Animal
eagle

ABOVE: *When the moon is passing through Scorpio, feelings will run deep, and destructive attitudes and explosive arguments are more likely occurrences. This is not the time to talk about important or sensitive issues, but to get on with some positive activity like decorating or gardening instead.*

ABOVE: *When the moon is passing through Sagittarius, things may not go according to plan, taking different turns to the ones planned for or expected. It is a time to be adaptable and to think of other ways to achieve your goals. Any travel plans may well be highlighted or have to be changed.*

Moon in Sagittarius

Sagittarius moon people are gregarious, funny, witty and tactless. Often speaking without thinking, these people need to learn how to be sociable without putting their foot in it. Sagittarius moons are highly independent and individualistic, not worrying too much about what others think of them, since they hold quite a high opinion of their own abilities anyway. They are very able, but a lack of sensitivity can sometimes mean that they tread on other people as they climb or travel to the top. They are mentally agile, with a love of and a need for freedom, often championing causes and following political concerns for the benefit of other people. They rise to a challenge, but need to guard against carelessness, including carelessness with money. Gambling is a strong temptation when the moon is placed here. Sagittarius moons can be reckless and would benefit from learning to pay attention to detail.

They have a naturally carefree attitude, which sometimes borders upon restlessness if their intellect is not sufficiently stimulated. Their work needs to be stimulating and challenging, so that they can rise to the task. This moon placement can bring great wisdom, if the carefree attitude is tempered with sensibility.

They make good partners and are probably among the best parents in the zodiac. However, if things start to go wrong in a relationship you will not see Sagittarians for dust. They will have left already, looking for a more optimistic landscape in which to champion their causes. Generally happy people, they find it hard to stay where they feel uncomfortable.

Moon in Capricorn

People with their moon in Capricorn will be hard-working, perhaps even workaholics. They have an almost fanatical dedication to making money and becoming successful, often at the expense of personal relationships. If other areas of the astrological chart are well starred, they can become very wealthy and perhaps even famous. However, this placement is not an easy one, and lunar Capricorns often have to make sacrifices, putting their own emotional needs aside for the good of the family, children, or anyone apart from themselves, which can lead them to become martyrs, with a tendency to moan about their lot. Capricorn moons can suffer with allergies and skin complaints, and benefit from being spontaneous, especially at those times when the limitations of martyrdom are affecting their health.

Women with their moon in Capricorn often put their feelings aside and settle with a partner who will provide them with material security – because this is seen as a need with this placement. Capricorn moon men, on the other hand, will often connect with a woman who can further their career – planning everything to their best personal advantage. This is not a sign that is willing to take risks.

Emotions do not figure strongly with Capricorn moons, and there can be a tendency to aloofness and detachment. This is sometimes balanced with a warm and funny sense of humour that rises spontaneously and can help to balance the rather superior, rigid exterior so often presented to the outside world.

Parents of this moon sign expect their children to work hard and do well and often need to accept their children for who they really are.

Stones
onyx

Flower
pansy

Animal
goat

ABOVE: *When the moon is passing through Capricorn, it is a good time to work on your finances, and attend to any practical matters. Capricorn men and women set great store by financial security and advancement and will put aside emotional matters, if necessary, to further this.*

ABOVE: *When the moon is passing through Aquarius, there will be an increase in creative and metaphysical ideas, with the opportunity to perform charitable acts. This phase of the moon is a good time to celebrate life; to have a party, or to invite some friends over for inspiring conversations and to share ideas.*

Moon in Aquarius

People with their moon in Aquarius can be highly original thinkers and extremely creative, often following a career in the performing or creative arts. They are interesting, unusual and will have many fascinating friends. However, Aquarius moons must guard against careless talk or flippant actions at times when life is too dull or humdrum for them. Although friendly and well-meaning, these people are not always the wisest when it comes to tact and diplomacy. They need to find a balance between innovative ideas and practical actions, and to avoid getting carried away with the next brilliant brainwave before it proves to be workable. They are outspoken and inventive. As lovers of freedom, they are often drawn to improving society in some way. Aquarius moons need for independence runs very deep, and they really hate to be tied down.

Aquarius moons have an interest in metaphysical issues, the occult and supernatural phenomena. They frequently present mysterious and magnetic qualities that draw the unusual to them. They can tend to be secretive and difficult to fathom because of this rather enigmatic predisposition. They are unpredictable, never quite reacting as expected, and sometimes causing confusion as a result. Being highly original, they need to ensure that they stay well grounded in material matters and in business concerns. Nervous tension can affect their health, especially anything to do with the eyes and lower body.

Moon in Aquarius parents are double-sided. They give strong moral support, but on the flip side expect their children to be independent at a relatively young age.

Stones
jet

Flower
snowdrop

Animal
swallow

Moon in Pisces

People with their moon in Pisces are extremely sensitive, and often psychic, with a natural intuitive ability. Being kind, compassionate and understanding, they are frequently drawn to working in humanitarian occupations, such as nursing, social work and healing.

They also seek out spiritual experiences. Because the moon in this placement can make them feel things so deeply, it can lead to lack of confidence, and they will try to find ways of reducing their insecurity by means of spiritual or mystical practices. There is also a creative streak in lunar Pisceans, and once they have gained confidence in their abilities, they have the potential to be extremely successful.

They see life as far more than material, and give a great deal to those in need, often at personal cost. However, this moon sign can also be dishonest, not because of any malice, but because of the fear of conflict, and a desire to limit any personal confrontations. Pisces moons can tend to put things off, making all kinds of excuses, but with the right kind of encouragement and positive input, they have the ability to make a great contribution to society. Being romantic by nature and soft at heart, they do require strong and positive partners, who will understand the Piscean sensitivity and vulnerability, and who will return in full the contributions to any partnership. It is easy to abuse the goodwill of Piscean moons, or to misunderstand their deep emotional nature.

Pisces moon parents are kind and sensitive to their children's needs, but sometimes lean on them for support. However, despite that, they will stand by their children through good times as well as bad

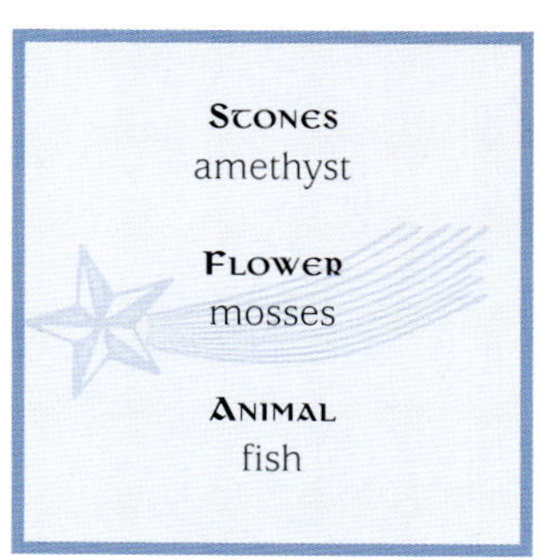

Stones
amethyst

Flower
mosses

Animal
fish

ABOVE: *When the moon is passing through Pisces, guard against any excessive emotional outbursts or a tendency to indulge yourself in your feelings, especially any negative or depressive tendencies. Keep the atmosphere lighthearted if you can, and always try to be both creative and positive.*

The Lunar Wheel of the Year

In Aryan mythology, the moon is the oldest recorded way of measuring time. Ancient civilizations calculated their significant festivals and activities according to the lunar cycles of the year. Our present Gregorian calendar is calculated according to the position of the earth in relation to the sun – measuring the length of a solar day – rather than by the far less predictable monthly cycle of the moon. Although it is more complicated, many cultures, such as Hebrew and Muslim, still have the means to calculate time by the moon.

For Buddhists, too, full and new moons are extremely important times, because they believe that the Buddha was born, achieved enlightenment and died during the period of the full moon. They still use a lunar calendar today, and one of their biggest annual festivals, Losar (New Year), begins on the February full moon.

A lunar year is calculated by months rather than by days (the moon gives its name to "month"), and each month incorporates the new, full, waning and dark aspect of the moon. The length of a lunar month is actually 29 days, 12 hours, 44 minutes and 28 seconds.

Several of our solar festivals were originally lunar festivals, hence their appearance in the lunar wheel of the year. Easter is still calculated according to when a particular full moon falls in the year. The Celtic celebrations of Imbolc (celebrated on 1 February) and Beltane (1 May) were also dedicated to the moon.

Some days are dedicated to moon goddesses. One of Diana's festivals is called the Ides of May, and it falls at the time of the May full moon. At this time, women

LEFT: *The Celts marked their festivals from the rising of the moon on the evening before the day of a particular event, and often lit ceremonial fires to honour them.*

LEFT: *Grottos, wells, springs and streams are all sacred to the moon. The traditional art of well-dressing honours the spirit of a place and its life-giving waters.*

would clean and tidy grottos, streams and water holes, and then wash the water over themselves as an act of cleansing and to encourage personal fertility. Diana is also venerated at the Harvest moon. Hecate, a moon goddess of the dark aspect, has her annual festival day on 13 August. This is the time when ancient peoples would call for her blessing on fair weather so that the harvest could be brought in safely.

The moon is honoured in many cultures. Zhong Qiu Jie is an autumnal lunar festival held by the Chinese, when offerings are made and celebrations abound to honour a bountiful harvest.

The lunar cycle is celebrated by pagans in the form of "full moon esbats". These ceremonies involve celebrating the full moon and sharing a feast, after any requests or dedications have been made, to signify the great abundance of the mother aspect of the moon and her ripeness at the full phase, the most powerfully fertile. In many ancient cultures, torches were lit to direct the rays of the moon down to the earth, to ensure her continued influence upon crops, childbirth, and fair weather.

Lunar Festivals of the Year

30 November eve	Festival of Hecate: weather
20/21 December eve	Winter Solstice – Celtic festival of the stars: light and life
1 February	Imbolc: rejuvenation, fertility
7 February	Festival of Selene
12 February	Festival of Diana
15 March	Festival of Cybele
20 March	Festival of Isis
20 March eve	Festival of Eostre (Easter): fertility
31 March	Festival of all Lunar Goddesses
1 May	Beltane/May Day: fertility, warmth and light
9 May	Festival of Artemis
26–31 May	Diana's Ides of May: fertility, abundance
21 June eve	Festival of Ceridwen
13 August eve	Festival of Hecate: weather and thanksgiving
September full moon eve	Festival of Candles/Harvest moon: crop yield
31 October eve	Festival of Hecate: remembrance of ancestors

The Moon's Phases

Before the advent of calendars, the king (or "moonman") was responsible for watching the moon's cycle and informing the tribal members when the new moon arrived, so that activities associated with the crescent could begin. He would continue to watch throughout the lunar month, informing members of each new phase. Any ceremonies, although led by the tribal chief, were always presided over by women, who were considered the potentizers of the moon's energy.

Traditionally, the moon has four phases: new, full, waning and dark. In ancient civilizations, the moon was considered to have three faces: the crescent, the full and the waning/dark. These three faces were embodied in the maiden, mother and crone of the Triple Goddess.

ABOVE: *The first quarter of the moon's cycle begins with the new moon, and lasts until only half of the moon is visible.*

The New Moon

Associated with Artemis, the new moon heralds the beginning of a new cycle, and is the time in magic when new opportunities can be seized. On the magic circle, the new moon is placed in the east – the place of the moon- rise and the place of a rising dawn. This slender beauty is seen as young and vulnerable, filled with the potential of a full moon to come, but as yet unrealized. The new moon is the maiden, the innocent, the conception, and this is a good time to work on health and personal growth, and to put plans into action for the month ahead. The new moon-time lasts for approximately three days of the first quarter.

LEFT: *Artemis is often shown many-breasted to indicate her ability to nourish and nurture new life.*

The first quarter is a time of expansion, development and growth, and can still be used for the same purposes as the new moon, as long as you make sure that you have completed your groundwork.

The way to recognize a new moon is to check that her "horns" are facing to the left. During the first quarter, you will see up to half of the moon's surface illuminated and, again, this will be her right-hand side.

The Full Moon

The full moon is the moon at her fullest and ripest. Represented by Isis, Selene, and Diana, among others, she is the embodiment of fertility, abundance and illumination. She is the moon at her most powerfully feminine and so is the

LEFT: *Symbolically the horse is a spirit animal able to carry you to the realms of the moon's magic and mystery. Call upon a spirit horse to help you on any magical journeys you may wish to take.*

fruit-bearer, the one who can encourage any seeds to grow. The full moon can be called upon to give fertility in the fields, as well as fertility of the body, and also for safe journeys across water. The most potent time for full-moon magic occurs in the three days prior to a full moon and at the actual time of the full moon. This is the second quarter. In full-moon ceremonies, the high priestess draws down the energies of a full moon into herself, embodying the great mystery of the feminine, by adopting the pentagram position within a sacred circle she has cast. Having drawn down the energies, she can be filled and refreshed, so that she has the strength to complete the next cycle of events in her life and the life of her community. Having drawn down the moon, the priestess can call for assistance for others, ask for blessings and healings for those in need and empower any of her own wishes. The full moon is also well known as the time of moon madness, or "lunacy" (from luna, the moon). The powerful energy of a full moon can trigger such things as epilepsy, as well as increasing the potential for accidents. People vulnerable to the influence of the full moon will feel more emotionally or mentally shaky at this time. In the female reproductive cycle, the full moon is the time of ovulation.

The Waning/Dark Moon

This moon is ruled by Hecate – a goddess of magic, sorcery and wisdom – Cybele and Ceridwen. The waning moon is the time when things can be cast away, let go of and released. It is also the time when insights can be gained. This is the power time for healings. Be aware that these goddesses are powerful. The days of the waning moon are called the third quarter (when the left-hand side of the moon is illuminated and the right-hand side is dark). After this period, the moon enters the rising power time of the fourth quarter, which is the last phase of the lunar cycle. This is a necessary part of the circle of Luna, when things can retreat into themselves, sink back into the earth, and rest for a while before the pull of the new moon draws everything out of itself again.

ABOVE: *The waning moon, ruled by Hecate, can be celebrated with candles, dragon charms and hands and feet decorated with red henna.*

In sorcery, the dark moon is the time of black magic, especially during the winter months, when the light on the earth is low. However, it is the most potent time for gaining understanding and should ideally be spent in contemplation, meditation and preparation, seeking the spiritual guidance of Isis, mother goddess of the moon, or of Sophia, the holy lady of wisdom. A dark moon is not the time for action unless it is of a banishing nature, and this is best done during the waning moon, the first to fourth day after the full moon, and not on the nights of true darkness, unless you really know what you are doing.

Hecate as a goddess of the underworld is symbolized with snakes for hair, like Medusa the Gorgon. She carries a torch and is attended by hounds. Hecate is also the goddess of crossroads, which is possibly why wrongdoers were strung up on gallows that were traditionally erected at crossroads. They were left to Hecate, goddess of the dark moon.

LEFT: *Early Christian women continued the tradition of praying to the moon rather than to God for favours.*

Circle of Luna

This is an approximation of the moon's cycle and her most active times in each quarter. Read the chart from new moon to new moon.

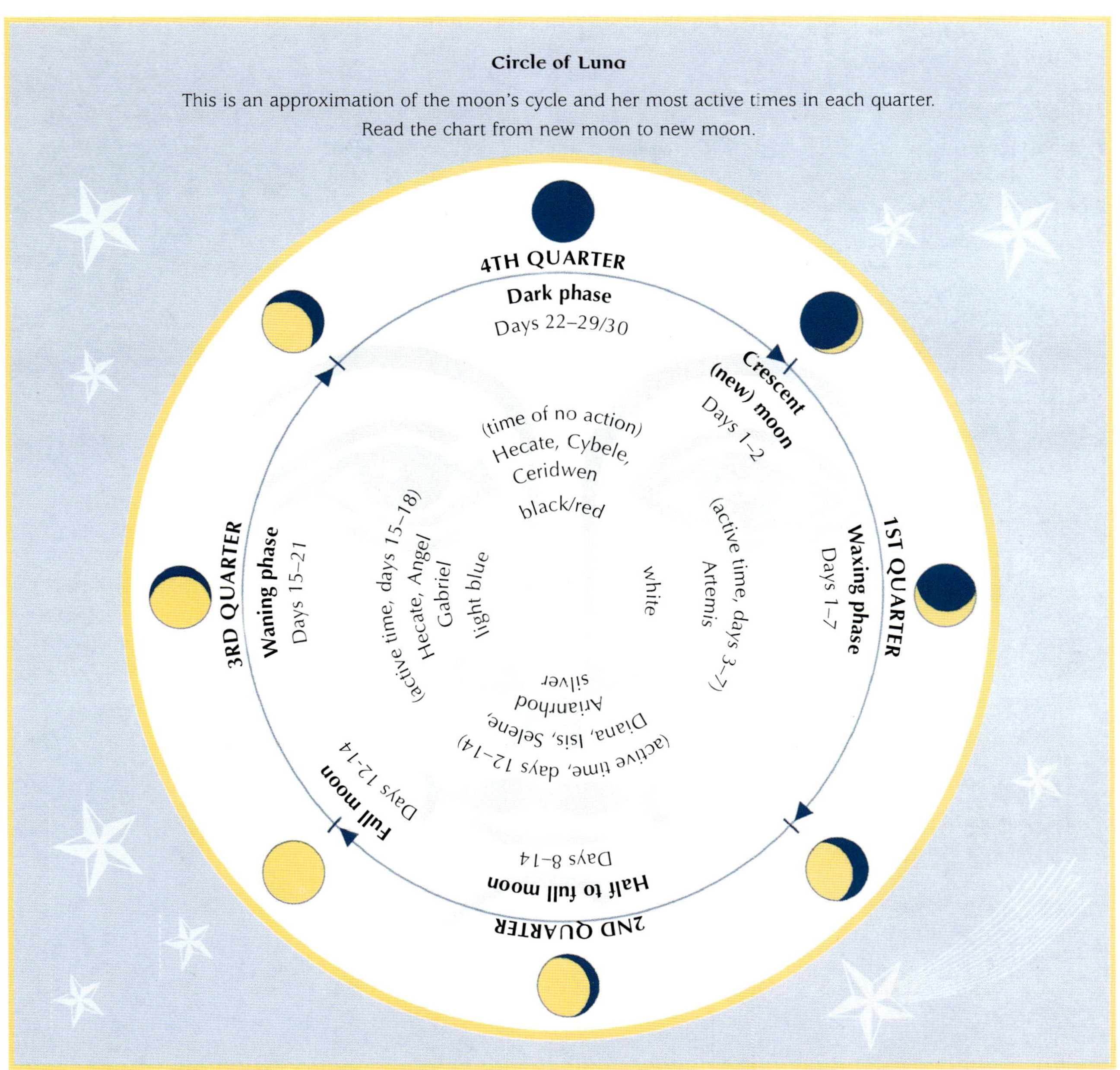

The Moon and Women

As the protector and guardian of women, the moon has long been associated with the female reproductive cycle. Many ancient civilizations performed fertility rituals and celebrated the moon at annual festivals dedicated to the goddess, to seek her help and favour with conception.

The female menstrual cycle mirrors the cycle of the moon in duration. The Latin word *mens*, meaning both mind and moon, is the basis for our word menstruation. The time of ovulation is likely to occur during a full moon. Women, the bearers of life, were seen by ancient civilizations as children of the moon goddess. Women can be very powerful, if their deep intuition is blended with spiritual wisdom. The full cycle of Luna must be travelled if wisdom is to be found. This can be achieved quite easily with meditation and devotion to the heart.

Within the heart of all women is the cycle of love. A woman generally finds it easy to nourish and care for others, to devote her life to beauty and harmony, and to speak from feeling rather than intellect. This reflects her "brightmoon" phase. Then there is the part of a woman that is jealous, possessive, scheming, vengeful, malicious, premenstrual – her "darkmoon" phase. During their menstruation, women are extremely sensitive and highly perceptive. Many ancient civilizations considered them too powerful when they were on their "moontime", and it was common for women to remove themselves from the rest of the tribe. Though this is not practised in modern societies, it may still be a good idea to set time aside to go within and use each "moontime" as a time to let go of the past cycle, and to allow the flow to cleanse and take away any problems or difficulties, thus making way for the new.

ABOVE: *Some ancient civilizations perceived the moon as masculine, and later as hermaphrodite – both male and female. More recently, largely because of changes in our religious structure, she is considered female and is depicted as such in works of art.*

Once wisdom spills into her heart, a woman passes the highest initiation and the lunar cycle takes on its greater perspective. No longer dictated to by emotions, but rather by insight and discrimination, no longer attached, but rhythmical, no longer selfish or jealous, but unconditionally compassionate, the wise woman has an extraordinary power.

Like women, the moon has cycles. Both of them possess the ability to generate the right conditions for new life and to continue to nurture it.

OPPOSITE: *A woman is a natural healer. When a child hurts itself, she automatically kisses or rubs it better; when a child cannot sleep, she sings or rocks it rhythmically. The moon and music are intimately linked, as is rhythmical movement (ebb and flow), underlining the correlation between the moon's wisdom and the ability of women to fulfil this role.*

The Moon and the Weather

The moon has a profound effect upon the earth's climate and atmosphere. She also affects the electromagnetic field that surrounds the earth, creating changes in atmospheric pressure that bring variations in the weather. Continuing research into the moon's effect upon earth's magnetic field, carried out since the 1960s, has shown that the full moon increases the incidence of meteorites falling to earth, and also affects the amount of ozone in the atmosphere.

The earth's magnetic field changes enough, during the monthly cycle of the moon, to affect not only the weather but our health as well, since human beings are sensitive to magnetism. The old wives' tale of feeling things "in one's bones" and our rheumatic aches and pains can be a valid interpretation of increased dampness in the air. The moon is known to influence rainfall, to raise storms, tidal flows, earthquakes, hurricanes and volcanic eruptions. Increases in these events have all been recorded just after a full moon. This aspect of the moon's power has psychological effects too. Mental instability increases dramatically during any very unsettled or stormy weather.

In severe drought, tribal people would make an offering of precious water to the moon, or milk a cow and offer the fluid in her honour. Clay balls were often flung at the full moon to encourage rain (clay being excellent at retaining water).

Foretelling the Weather

- ☆ Moon lore states that a new moon always brings a change in the weather, and if the horns of the moon are sharp, it indicates windy weather.
- ☆ A crescent moon cupped and on its back means rain will fall.
- ☆ If you can see a star close to the moon, you can expect to have "wild weather".
- ☆ A bright full moon heralds good weather, and a mottled full moon will bring rain.

RIGHT: *If you see a single halo around a full moon, you can expect mild breezes; the more halos present, the greater the increase in the wind. Volcanic eruptions frequently occur just after a full moon.*

The Blue Moon

The old saying "once in a blue moon" refers to a time when two moons occur in the same calendar month, a rather rare occurrence. During the twentieth century, for example, there were only 40 blue moons. A blue moon appears about every two and a half years, usually during a month that has 31 days in it. It signifies a special time: a doubling of the moon's powers during the month in which she appears. Considered unlucky by some, the blue moon is, in fact, a magical moon, when long-term objectives can be set. So, a blue moon can be used to sow seeds for your future, giving them time to germinate and grow until the next blue moon rises. But you should be careful if you intend to weave magic during a blue moon. Be very clear about what you ask for, because this moon will be potent, doubling your wish and intent.

ABOVE: *Check for two moons in one month in a lunar calendar, the second moon is the blue moon and is twice as potent as a normal full moon.*

People born during a blue moon have great potential, but may have difficulty bringing their gifts into action. Their strengths are also their weaknesses, and blue moon people have to learn how to harness their powers for the benefit of themselves and those they meet in life.

A blue moon also increases the lunar influence on the weather, with a high probability that rainfall, storms and exceptionally high tides will be more prevalent than usual during that month.

ABOVE: *Because of the power she brings to those born during this time, the blue moon's magic needs to be understood. Blue moon people may have a tendency to moodiness, volatility and emotionalism, as well as the gentler attributes of compassion, caring, sensitivity and natural intuition.*

LUNAR GARDENING

Because the moon has such a strong influence over crop yields, for centuries farmers, agriculturists and gardeners have used the lunar phases when planting, tending and harvesting crops. This is done by observing the correct phase of the moon for a particular activity, and also by adhering to the sign of the zodiac that it is passing through. There are four lunar phases to be considered. The moon is increasing in influence between the new and full phases (brightmoon) and decreasing in influence between the waning and dark phases (darkmoon). As a general rule, the first and second quarter are the most auspicious times for planting and tending cereal crops, leafy crops and annual plants and flowers. The third quarter is good for root crops and bulbs, trees, shrubs and rhubarb. The moon's fourth quarter is the best time for garden maintenance: for weeding, cultivation and the removal of pests, especially when the moon is in Aries, Gemini, Leo, or Aquarius.

ABOVE: *Plant sweetcorn during the new moon to encourage fleshy corns.*

You can start a compost heap during the darkmoon time, or harvest and dry ever-lasting flowers and herbs, especially if the moon is in a fire sign. A water moon is the best time to irrigate fields and gardens. If, to begin with, you find it a little too complicated to check the zodiac signs for your gardening tasks, you can simply follow the moon's phases of waxing and waning.

NEW MOON

Seeds of plants that flower above the ground should be sown at the new moon. This is also the time for farmers to sow cereals such as barley, and for the garden to be planted with asparagus, broccoli, Brussels sprouts, sweetcorn, cabbage, melons, cauliflower, celery, courgettes, cress, horseradish, kohlrabi, leeks, peas, peppers, parsley, spinach, squash and tomatoes. This is also the time for fertilizing and feeding anything that you wish to flourish.

ABOVE: *Bulbs, root crops, perennials and biennials should be tended and planted during the darkmoon phase.*

LEFT: *Lunar gardening doesn't mean gardening by night, but by her phases through the month.*

LEFT AND BELOW: *Tend leafy plants and feed the garden well during the new moon. This is also the best time for watering and fertilizing.*

Full Moon

Around the full moon is the time to plant watery or fleshy plants such as marrows and cucumbers. The moon is at her most influential at this time over the water element. This is also a good time for harvesting the leaves, stems, or seeds of herbs for drying, especially when the moon is transiting a fire sign. It is important to pick your herbs on a dry day, so that the parts to be harvested will not rot when stored. The best time to harvest is just before midday. String the stems together and hang them upside down in an airy, cool but dry atmosphere, until ready for use.

Pick mushrooms at the full moon. The best time is just after dawn, when the dew is still on the grass. Take them home and have them for breakfast. Do remember that some fungi are poisonous: be very careful to ensure that you pick only edible mushrooms. Get an expert to guide you, or consult a good reference book and do not eat anything you are unsure about.

Elemental Gardening Table

Gardening by the moon's phases is simple once you have mastered the basic principles. Just ensure that you are within the correct moon phase for a particular gardening task, and that the moon is passing through an appropriate sign. For details on the moon's phases and when it is passing through a particular star sign, you will need to refer to a lunar almanac. Then check the chart below to discover which zodiacal sign is most appropriate for each activity.

Air	Water
Gemini (barren and dry) Weeding, clearing, pest control	**Cancer (very fruitful and moist)** Best sign for planting, sowing and cultivating
Libra (moist) Plant fruit trees, fleshy vegetables, root vegetables	**Scorpio (very fruitful and moist)** Very good sign for planting, sowing and general cultivation, especially vine fruits; start a compost heap
Aquarius (barren and dry) Garden maintenance, weeding and pest control	**Pisces (very fruitful and moist)** Excellent for planting, especially root crops

Fire	Earth
Aries (barren and dry) Weeding, clearing, garden maintenance	**Taurus (fertile and moist)** Plant root crops and leafy vegetables
Leo (barren and dry) Bonfires, ground clearance, weeding	**Virgo (barren and moist)** Cultivation, weeding and pest control
Sagittarius (barren and dry) Plant onions, garden maintenance	**Capricorn (productive and dry)** Good for root vegetables

ABOVE: *Plant, feed and prune flowers, especially biennials and perennials, during the darkmoon phase.*

Incidentally, the full moon is also an excellent time for baking bread. The influence of the full moon proves the yeast better, and encourages the dough to rise.

Waning and Dark Moon

The waning moon is the time in the moon's cycle for root vegetables, peas and beans, and garlic. Anything undertaken during this time will benefit underground development or retard growth. This is therefore an excellent time to mow the grass, when its return growth will be slowed, or to plough and turn the soil. Gather and harvest crops during the waning moon, especially in late summer, the traditional harvest time. This is an excellent time to prune trees, roses and shrubs, and to water the garden. Making jams and pickles should also be done during a waning moon, for best results.

Crops that are suited to planting during the waning moon are endive, carrots, garlic, onions, potatoes, radishes, beetroot and strawberries.

All flowering bulbs, biennials, and perennials should be planted during this time, especially when the moon is in a water sign. Saplings also benefit from being planted during the waning moon, when she is in Cancer, Scorpio, Pisces or Virgo.

The principles of lunar gardening take a while to adjust to, but soon you will find that your flowers bloom brighter, crops grow more succulent and flavoursome, and trees have stronger roots. In fact your whole garden will benefit from this ancient and effective way of gardening.

ABOVE: *Harvesting your vegetables should be done during a waning or dark moon.*

ABOVE: *Radishes, carrots and other roots should be planted during a waning moon.*

ABOVE: *Farmers should concentrate on cereal crops during the brightmoon phase.*

A Water Garden Feature

Diana's festival days fall upon the May and September full moons. At one of these times, you may like to perform a water ceremony in your garden or at a local waterfall, well, stream, lake or river, or on the seashore. This idea is inspired by the ancient art of well-dressing, when communities "dress" their local source of water with a plaque decorated with symbols, flowers, corn, rice, stones and twigs, placing it by the water as a way of giving thanks. This is an excellent group activity and can be great fun to do with children. Any lunar totem can be included in the design, such as a dove, cat, or owl, or perhaps some circles and spirals.

Perform the ceremony two days before the full moon. As you place your plaque next to the water, you may like to say a prayer to the moon, asking for her blessing and protection for the year to come. Use your own words, as they come.

You Will Need

- potter's clay
- rolling pin
- piece of wood cut to shape
- knife
- stick or skewer
- flower petals, leaves, twigs, corn, rice, pasta, shells and pebbles
- toothpick (optional)
- wet cloth

1 Roll out the clay to about 6 mm/¼ in. Trace around your chosen wooden shape and cut it out from the clay with the knife.

2 Press the clay down firmly on to the wood, then mark out your design on the surface.

3 Fill in the design using petals, leaves and other elements, pushing them into the clay with your fingernails or a toothpick. Cover your work with a wet cloth when you are not working on it, to keep the clay soft.

Lunar Plants

The moon, like the planets, has particular plants that come under her influence. These have been used in ceremonies and rituals to the moon goddess, and were also depicted in traditional art and sculpture. Flowers of the moon include all the aquatic plants, such as water lilies, seaweed, lotus and watercress, as well as jasmine and poppy. All flowers that are white or that blossom at night, such as night-scented stock, come under the regulation of the moon.

LEFT: *On the night of the new or full moon, you may like to arrange a vase of moon flowers and light two white (new moon) or silver (full moon) candles.*

Trees associated with the moon include the willow, a tree that thrives near water, the aspen, eucalyptus, pear, plum and lemon. The willow is also known as the moon's wishing tree. Calling for favour with a willow tree by tying white, silver or light-blue ribbons to her branches on lunar festival days can help to draw attention to a wish.

LEFT: *Make a magical wand from a branch of willow, the moon's wishing tree.*

Another moon tree is sandalwood. Associated with protection, purification and healing, chippings of the bark of *Santalum album* are used in ceremonies requiring these qualities. It has a beautifully calming and soothing smell.

Camphor is a white resinous gum, extracted from *Cinnamonum camphora*, a tree found in China, Japan and other parts of east Asia. It is one of the aromatic fragrances associated with the moon. Camphor has a strong and distinct smell, and has cooling qualities rather like menthol. Camphor's cool and yet penetrating property brings it close to the lunar mysteries. By strewing it on the ground, or burning it ritually, people of the ancient world felt they were able to attract the favours and attentions of the goddess.

The Moon and Numerology

In numerology the moon is associated with the number two, a highly feminine number, although in magic she is assigned the number nine. Any years or months that add up to the number two will come under the influence of the moon. Moon years are romantic, creative, unpredictable, deep and intuitive, with a need to bring harmony and stability. However, if the negative aspects of the moon prevail during a number two year, there will be a tendency for depression, cruelty, and possessiveness.

To discover if you are in a moon year, take the four figures and add them together. (For example, the year 2090 becomes 2 + 9 = 11; 1 + 1 = 2.)

Leading up to the present millennium, the year 1999, when broken down into a single number, becomes the number one (1 + 9 + 9 + 9 = 28; 2 + 8 = 10; 1 + 0 = 1). The sun is represented by 1.

The year 2000, however, adds up to the number two. Thus, being a lunar year, it heralded an important time to get in touch with inner feelings and emotions, to be with the family, to enhance productivity, and to promote the good of the whole. As the wheel of time turns from sun to moon, so the less predictable but fruitful moon holds sway.

Moon people (those whose name or date of birth adds up to the number two) are dedicated parents, have a need for security and emotional reassurance, and have close links with nature and water, in a positive or negative way. Darker aspects of this personality include jealousy, manipulation, deception and vindictiveness. "Two" people need to guard against being two-faced.

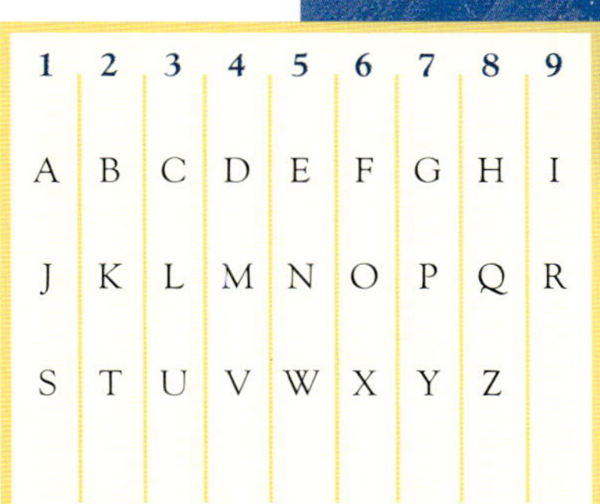

1	2	3	4	5	6	7	8	9
A	B	C	D	E	F	G	H	I
J	K	L	M	N	O	P	Q	R
S	T	U	V	W	X	Y	Z	

ABOVE: *The strongest lunar influence will be felt by the individual whose birth date adds up to the number two.*

LEFT: *The lunar name will play a less significant part but will still affect the qualities of a personality.*

Turning Names into Numbers

To discover if you are a moon person, take the letters of your chosen name or your birth date and translate them into numbers using this chart. This can be done with either your full name, your first name or a chosen name that you use in place of your given name. "Sarah", for example, becomes 2 (1 + 1 + 9 + 1 + 8 = 20; 2 + 0 = 2). Sarahs will feel a connection with the attributes of the moon. To work out if you are a moon child, add up the numbers of your birth date (for example, 2.4.1967 becomes 29: 2 + 9 = 11, 1 + 1 = 2).

Lunar Colours

Like the planets in our solar system, the moon has colours that are traditionally associated with her. Use and wear the appropriate lunar colours when you are performing ceremonies during the various phases of the moon, or simply to maintain your connection with the moon's phases and increase your awareness of her cycles and influence.

White has always been associated with purity and innocence and therefore represents the crescent or new moon. White and milky stones, like the moonstone, opal or milky quartz, are also associated with the new moon. White candles should be burned when working during this phase – for example, to call for new opportunities.

Silver, both as a colour and as a metal, has the most favourable lunar associations, because of its coolness and fluidity. Silver jewellery, especially when worn during the new- to full-moon phase, can enhance all the magical qualities of the moon and help to connect the intuitive self with lunar energies.

LEFT: *Burn two silver candles when working with general moon magic, such as a full moon celebration, or esbats, as they are known in pagan circles.*

Light blue has long been associated with the Virgin Mary, a lady of the moon, and is a very healing colour. It can soothe, calm and cool heated emotions, illness or burns and stings. Once appropriate medical attention has

LEFT: *White stones and flowers will increase your connection to the new or crescent moon. Lilies are particularly linked to the moon. Burn some white candles when performing any lunar ceremonies in this phase.*

LEFT: *Float three, seven or nine light-blue candles in a clear glass bowl filled with spring water for healing ceremonies and during the waning moon.*

ABOVE: *Black and red are the colours of the darkmoon goddesses. Although traditionally described as the time for dark magic, it is also the peak time for women to connect to their innate wisdom.*

been administered, visualize a light-blue colour bathing a specific area, or the whole person, and you will notice a marked reduction in the symptoms.

Black is a much maligned colour in some quarters. This is the colour of the darkmoon, when the inner world can speak most clearly. It is associated with Hecate, goddess of death and the underworld. Black is a silent, inward colour, so can be worn as protection or when seeking insight. It is the colour of power and identity. Burn white candles during the darkmoon phase, and meditate in black clothes or cloaked in a black cloth to help you travel inwards.

Traditionally, red is put with the full moon, but here it is placed with the dark moon because red has not only long been associated with the underworld but also represents the female. In the cycle of Luna, menstruation would occur during the waning/darktime of the moon.

ABOVE: *If you feel drawn to setting up an altar to the full moon, you may like to use a light-blue cloth, silver candles, sandalwood incense and wild water meadow or riverside flowers, adding any other lunar totems and crystals you wish. Remember to be careful of poisonous plants and not to pick protected species.*

The Moon and the Tarot

Tarot cards are believed to have originated in Egypt although, like most inherited systems of divination, we cannot be certain of their real origin. In medieval times, the moon was depicted as Fortuna, the Wheel of Fortune in the tarot deck. This card depicts the ups and downs of life, the cycles that represent life's changing fortunes, sometimes hard and sometimes easy. Like the Wheel of Fortune, the moon is ever-changing, and reminds us that life ebbs and flows.

The moon card in the tarot deck is numbered 18 (1 + 8). This gives the number nine, which is the magical number of the moon. Nine denotes the completion of a cycle and so signifies that a new beginning is about to occur. If you draw this card, it tells you that intuition and perception will be your greatest allies in the days to come. Trust your feelings, and take a little time before making any decisions of a life-changing nature.

LEFT: *The tarot can be a very powerful means of connecting with the intuitive forces of the moon, acting as a focus of attention for perception to unfold.*

BELOW: *The moon in the tarot traditionally symbolizes deception, fear, and uncertainty, often found in a spread where someone is having (or thinking of having) a secret affair. It can also indicate that an important change is about to occur.*

This is a card of feelings and emotions, of all aspects of the feminine, and so may represent an emotional or psychic understanding or change, especially if time is spent in contemplation of the moon's present message. It also conveys a warning that emotionalism and negative reactions that are not tempered with any higher wisdom can lead you into emotional confusion. This card signifies that you are completing one cycle and not yet beginning another – so can raise fears, doubts, and upsets. Don't get carried away with fantasies; stay practical and well grounded in reality, and trust that as one door closes, so another opens.

Take the moon card from the deck and hold it so that the picture is touching your third eye (in the centre of your forehead). Close your eyes and melt into the card, noting symbols, images and feelings that arise.

MAKING A LUNAR TAROT CARD

One way to deepen your connection with the moon is to make your own lunar card. This can be done with paints, crayons, collage or any medium you want to work in. Make up a design of your own that represents the moon for you, just sit quietly with paper and pencil and allow the ideas to form. When your moon card is completed, you can place it upon your altar, and meditate upon it, to help to bring insights and revelations. If you feel you cannot draw, cut out pictures and glue them to the card instead. Make the card just before the new moon, to ensure that your intuition and perception increase as the new moon grows.

YOU WILL NEED

- scissors
- white card
- ruler
- silver pen
- paints or crayons
- paintbrush
- glue
- selection of the following: silver glitter, silver and/or blue sequins, stars and moon sequin shapes
- pictures of moon animals, birds, trees, crystals, moon flowers, water
- white feathers (especially dove or duck)
- blue ribbons
- silver tape
- blue or silver candles
- matches

1 Cut out a piece of card measuring 9 x 13 cm/ 3½ x 5 in and draw your chosen design on it. You can make the card bigger if you feel confident to do so.

2 Paint your design or glue on your chosen collage materials. Let your mind be led by imagination and creativity as you make up your design.

3 When it is complete, place the card on your altar or special area. Light two blue or silver candles. Meditate on the images for three nights. Make a note of any dreams.

A Lunar Talisman

In magic, the moon is associated with the number nine. The "kamea", or magic square, of the moon adds up to the number nine in all directions and can be used in magic to connect with the powers and gifts that the moon provides.

When making a lunar talisman, it is important to observe the correct timing: the new moon to the full moon is the time for drawing things to you; the full moon to the beginning of the dark moon is the time for releasing things. For example, if you are seeking new beginnings or fertility, use the new moon, whereas if you are asking for healing, use the waning time. The new to full phase of the moon is for growth and attraction. The waning to dark phase of the moon is for decrease and removal.

Place an attracting talisman in the light of the moon with a moonstone or white circular stone resting on top, until your wish is granted. Take a releasing talisman to a river or seashore on the first night after a full moon and place it in the water to be taken away. Watch it leave, and then turn away. Do not look back.

To make your talisman, you will first need to work out the sigil of your name. Convert your name into numerals using the Numerology Chart on page 171. For example, the name Isabel becomes the numbers 911253. Then trace the shape of those numbers on the kamea. Begin with a small circle, then draw a line connecting the numerals until you have a sigil, or pattern. Isabel would begin by joining nine to one, then one to two and so on. End the sigil with a line.

The Kamea of the Moon

A lunar kamea can be used to balance the emotions, to call for fertility, and to enhance perceptions and psychic abilities, as well as for journeys at night or over water.

37	78	29	70	21	62	13	54	5
6	38	79	30	71	22	63	14	46
47	7	39	80	31	72	23	55	15
16	48	8	40	81	32	64	24	56
57	17	48	9	41	73	33	65	25
26	58	18	50	1	42	74	34	66
67	27	59	10	51	2	43	75	35
36	68	19	60	11	52	3	44	76
77	28	69	20	61	12	53	4	45

37	78	29	70	21	62	13	54	5
6	38	79	30	71	22	63	14	46
47	7	39	80	31	72	23	55	15
16	48	8	40	81	32	64	24	56
57	17	48	9	41	73	33	65	25
26	58	18	50	1	42	74	34	66
67	27	59	10	51	2	43	75	35
36	68	19	60	11	52	3	44	76
77	28	69	20	61	12	53	4	45

LEFT: *Whenever your sigil runs consecutively through one number, represent this with a loop.*

Making a Lunar Talisman

A talisman is simply a written wish, and can take any form. This lunar talisman will call upon the power of the moon.

You Will Need

- 2 silver or white candles
- matches
- silver pen
- ruler
- 23 cm/9 in square of natural paper

1 Light your two silver or white candles, saying as you do so:
"Hail to you Levanah. I light these candles in your honour and ask for your assistance this night."

ABOVE: *Make your talisman on a Monday, the day of the moon, preferably after she has risen and during the correct phase for attracting or releasing.*

2 Draw a 5 cm/2 in square in the top left-hand corner of the piece of paper. Copy the sigil of your name (do not include any numbers) into the square. Write your wish in the remaining space.

3 Fold the four corners of the paper to the centre to make a diamond shape, then repeat twice more.

RIGHT: *Leave your talisman with a moonstone in the light of the increasing moon to draw her favour to your wish.*

Moon Crystals

The moon has been associated with particular sacred stones for thousands of years. Traditionally, white stones are associated with the waxing and full moon, and dark stones with the waning and dark aspects.

Certain crystals have a sympathetic resonance with the cool, subtle energies of the moon. These crystals can help to align your vibrations to hers, so inducing clearer dreams, clairvoyant awakening, deeper perceptions and emotional understanding. Some moon crystals have a balancing effect upon the menstrual cycle, some upon dreaming and yet others upon emotional health.

ABOVE: *You can take your crystals to lakes or the seashore during a full moon and cleanse them there in the water.*

Bright Moontime Crystals

White, clear or watery bright stones should be used for the new to full phase of the lunar cycle.

Celestite

In its blue or white varieties, celestite can help to link you to your spirit guides, to the beings of the light who help to illuminate your way in the dreamtime, so that gifts from the spirit can be given to you.

Moonstone

A moonstone crystal can be used to balance your hormonal cycle, to calm any unsettled emotions, especially if concerned with parenting issues, and also to induce lucid dreaming.

Aquamarine

An intense icy blue crystal, aquamarine makes an ideal dream crystal, tuning you into the rhythms of the sea and the depths of your own spirit, so that you can access divine wisdom and guidance.

Circular White Stones

As well as particular gems or crystals, any round white-coloured stones or pebbles can be used to represent the full moon, or increase your connections with her.

Azurite (right)

Known as the "stone of heaven", azurite can help attune your mind to the psychic world. It ranges in colour from dark blue to light blue, one of the lunar colours.

Clear Quartz (right)

A crystal that looks like frozen water, clear quartz has a strong affinity with the moon and can be used to enhance and direct the moon's rays in ceremonies of healing or invocation.

Pearls (below)

"Pearls of wisdom" are spoken of in the Bible. Pearls are symbolic of the moon because they are made in the sea. They represent purity, clarity and grace, and can be used to help enhance those qualities. The wearer is healthy if the pearls hold their soft sheen. Pearl flower essence can be used to balance the hormones and emotions, and to increase confidence in inner wisdom.

RIGHT: *Leave lunar crystals out for three days prior to a full moon so that they can become re-energized with lunar powers.*

Dark Moontime Crystals

Dark or cloudy stones are used to represent this phase of the moon's cycle, when insights can be gained, wisdom can be sought, and preparation made for the new moonrise.

Holey flint

A flint with a hole in can protect the wearer from night terrors and fears from negative thought forms. String one on a red thread and wear or carry it wherever you need to.

Jet

A deeply black mineral, formed from fossilized wood, jet is highly symbolic of the dark moon. Jet calms all the subtle bodies, clears a heavy head, and can help in the lifting of depression or gloominess. It is especially useful for clearing negative inner or outer environments where the build-up of tension is preventing sleep.

Citrine

A crystal of the sun, because of its vibrant amber colour, citrine has been included as a preventer of nightmares and night fears. It warms and soothes the mental and emotional body, so that you feel calm and relaxed enough to have a good night's sleep. Citrine can help to soothe children back to sleep.

Black Stones

Smooth, circular black or dark stones have also traditionally been associated with and used during the dark moon phase.

Keep an eye out for them on riverside or beach walks and then carry them with you whenever you are feeling confused or disorientated, as they will help to bring illumination.

Caring for Your Crystals

Crystals have the ability to attract, store or direct energy. If your crystal feels heavy, full and dull put it out on the night of a full moon and leave for four days so that it takes in some of the waning moon. This helps it to release excess energies. If the crystal feels empty and lifeless put it out in the new moon to help it restore its vitality. To find out what your crystal needs, sit with it quietly and you will sense what is the right thing to do.

The best way to clean lunar crystals is to hold the stones under running water then leave in moonlight to dry. You can also cleanse a crystal in the smoke from an incense or smudge stick, or use visualization by blowing over the stones as you imagine clearing the negatives, or bury the stones in the earth and leave for four days.

Casting a Brightmoon Circle

This ceremony can be performed every month to honour the moon, as the protector and guardian of women. When women cast the circle, it will refresh and rejuvenate them for the month to come, and for a man, it will have a symbolic rather than biological significance as he follows his own rhythms and cycles from the female within. The ceremony can be done outdoors or in, within two days leading up to a full moon.

You Will Need

- 13 circular stones, river stones or moon crystals
- salt
- aromatherapy burner
- matches
- jasmine essential oil
- 9 candles

1 Turning clockwise, put 12 of your chosen stones (these can be all different sizes) in a circle around you, beginning in the south. Put the last stone in the centre.

2 Sprinkle the stones with some salt. Light the burner and put in three drops of jasmine oil.

3 Place eight candles around the circle and one by the centre stone. As you light the candles, say, "Magna Dei, light of the night, I light these candles to guide your moonrays here. I ask you to come and bless this circle."

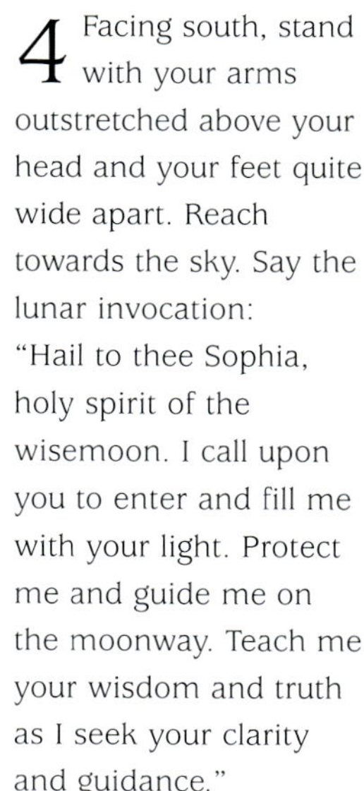

4 Facing south, stand with your arms outstretched above your head and your feet quite wide apart. Reach towards the sky. Say the lunar invocation: "Hail to thee Sophia, holy spirit of the wisemoon. I call upon you to enter and fill me with your light. Protect me and guide me on the moonway. Teach me your wisdom and truth as I seek your clarity and guidance."

5 Imagine yourself drawing down the powers of the moon into yourself. Allow yourself to be refreshed and re-filled with the feminine virtues of wisdom, beauty and grace. Let the moon bless your feelings and perceptions until you feel energized and content. Bring your arms down to your sides. Close your circle by saying "Thank you". Blow out your candles and dispose of organic ingredients outside.

Moon Medicines

Mother Moon holds important healing energies that can be called upon during her various phases: the new moon for health, vitality and regeneration; the full moon for fertility; the waning phase to remove the symptoms and ailments associated with general health problems. It is important to stress here that if you do have a concern about your health, you should consult a qualified medical practitioner.

Lunar medicine is made utilizing the light of either a new, full or waning moon. Being the mother figure of human-kind, the moon can empower medicines with healing and calming vibrations.

Timing is important, so make sure the moon is in the correct phase before you begin. You may find you have to wait a while for the correct phase of the moon's cycle, but please do stick to the guidelines outlined above. This will ensure that your medicine will contain the most appropriate vibrations for your needs.

RIGHT: *It is advisable to only make outdoor lunar medicines when the weather is clear and calm.*

Moon Dew Medicine

LEFT: *You can take moonstone flower essence to help to balance your menstrual cycle, following the instructions on the bottle.*

Another beautiful attribute of the moon is her connection with fertility. In ancient days, women would rise before dawn and go to the fields on the day of the full moon to bathe in the early morning moon dew. Washing down their bodies with the moisture of the early morning, they would call to Luna for her favours, either for a child or for fertile crops.

To bathe in moon dew yourself, all you need to do is to rise before dawn and go to a field or into the garden. Gather some dew into your hands by scraping them over the grasses and flowers and wipe down your face, hands and feet. If you have enough privacy, you may like to bathe your whole body. While washing, feel the moon caressing your skin, and the feminine influences permeating your body. Call to Mother Moon to bless and protect you, and ask her for what you need. Once you have finished your request or prayer, say thank you to her.

Lunar Medicine to Reduce Stress

To make a moon medicine that is helpful in times of emotional strain, you will need to perform this healing ceremony three nights after the first night of a full moon, after sunset. It can be performed outside on a calm night, or inside by the light of the moon.

You Will Need

- glass bowl
- 9 white nightlights
- matches
- moonstone
- spring water

1 Place the glass bowl on the floor in front of you, then position the nine night-lights in a circle around it.

2 Light the candles, starting with the one in the south, saying while you do so: "Hail to thee Levanah, Queen of Heaven. I call for your blessings and ask that your moonrays fill this essence with healing."

3 Put your crystal in the bowl and pour in the spring water until the crystal is completely covered. Leave it in place for at least three hours. Do not leave the nightlights burning unattended and replace any that burn out.

4 After three hours, blow out the nightlights, remove the crystal, pour the infusion into a glass and sip slowly while visualizing yourself being touched by the moon's rays.

Psychic Dreams

You can enhance your connection to the inner world of dreams by using an aquamarine crystal placed under your pillow as you sleep. Aquamarine crystals are quite easily obtainable from crystal suppliers and from some new-age shops. Store your dream crystal in a little pouch, made from a shimmery material in pale blue or silver and decorated with moon charms and sequins. Perform a dedication ceremony on the crystal before you start using it.

Making a Crystal Pouch

You Will Need

- 7.5 x 20 cm/3 x 8 in piece of fabric
- needle and cotton thread
- silver crescent or full-moon charm
- sequins in silver, blue and green
- small safety pin
- 2 x 20 cm/8 in lengths of thin blue or silver ribbon
- aquamarine crystal

1 To make the pouch, turn in and sew a narrow hem along both long edges on the wrong side of the fabric.

2 Sew your moon decorations and sequins on to the right side. Turn down a double 1 cm/½ in hem along the short edges, making a casing for the ribbon.

3 Fold the fabric in half, right sides together, and sew along the two long edges until you reach the casing. Leave the casing unsewn. Turn right sides out. Using a safety pin, thread a piece of ribbon through both sides of the casing and back to the starting point. Knot the ends. Repeat from the other side.

Awakening the Psychic

To empower your dreamtime with the moon's energies, place any moon-governed offering by the side of your bed, as an exchange for her help. This can be seashells, river stones, moon charms, or moon flowers for example, and then dedicate them to her with a personal prayer. This can be done on a monthly basis. If flowers are your offering, ensure you dispose of them with thanks and sensitivity.

LEFT: *The domain of sleep and dreams is governed by the moon. To ensure peaceful sleep during stressful times, place an amethyst in your crystal pouch.*

Dedicating your Crystal

Aquamarine is ideal to help develop psychic connections, but before you do this you can clear your dreamtime by first placing jet or citrine in your pouch. Place this under your pillow for a few nights during a waning moon until any nightmares or unsettled sleep patterns are gone.

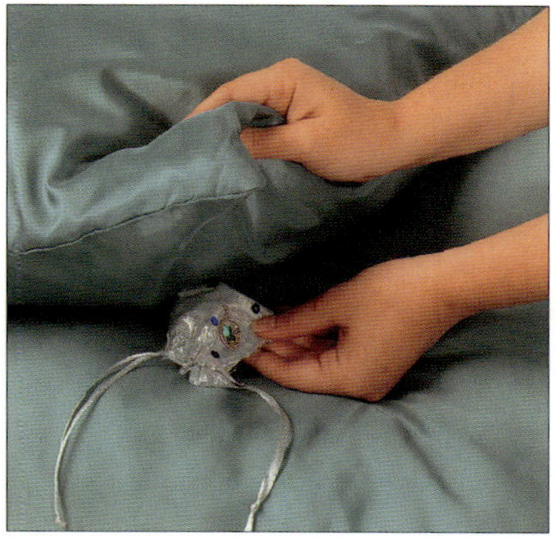

1 For your ceremony, choose a clear, calm night, just before or during the full-moon phase, especially when the moon is in a water sign (Cancer, Pisces or Scorpio). Dedicate your crystal just after sunset when the moon is visible to you indoors.

2 Hold the crystal up to the light of the moon, saying as you do so: "Hail to thee Levanah. I call to you to bring your blessings to this moon crystal, and ask you to fill it with your rays, that I may learn the wisdom of the dreamtime. Thank you."

3 Place your crystal in your dream pouch. Put it under your pillow for one month. Perceptive dreams should then enter your sleep. You can perform this ceremony of dedication for your dream crystal every month at the full moon, if you like, or every three months as a matter of course.

The Sacred Moon Tree

This mythical tree is a "tree of the gods", said to provide the fruits of immortality. The secrets of immortality are held by the moon rather than the sun, because she has the power over life, death and regeneration, owing to her influence on rhythms and cycles, as well as conception and germination. The sacred tree of the gods is therefore placed in her domain.

Past civilizations believed that the fruits of immortality actually grew upon this sacred tree on the moon, and ceremonies were ritually performed by Vedic priests of India, using an intoxicating milky juice extracted from the Soma plant, *Asclepias acida*. Soma was also the name of a Vedic god, equivalent to the Roman god Bacchus, and sc strong is the link with the moon that in post-Vedic writings, Soma is the name given to the moon itself.

Soma is known as the king of plants, because of its powerful link with the gods. By taking Soma, the holy people would also be able to connect with the deeper aspects of lunar wisdom, the wisdom that comes from deep within the psyche, and is innately feminine.

Female Wisdom

All women can relate to the feeling of "knowing" something about a future event, or of having strong gut feelings about a particular issue. Men can work on this feminine side of their personalities too by deepening the bond with the moon and honouring her presence in the night sky, especially when she is full. The highest initiation of Luna is one of wisdom, of allowing the psyche to influence action and to follow this inner voice. The great Wise Mother, beyond death, beyond the veil of illusion, holds these secrets of feminine spirituality. Soma from the sacred Moon Tree, therefore, represents both immortality and profound wisdom.

ABOVE: *Developing lunar awareness will help to increase trust in the more subtle aspects of the psyche, including perception, intuition and psychic understanding.*

Making a Moon Tree

You can make and decorate your own moon tree during the period coming up to and during the full-moon phase. You might like to make one for Christmas one year, in place of the traditional evergreen tree. Our traditional Christmas tree is hung with baubles to represent the planets continuing to encircle the earth throughout the coming year. This moon tree has been decorated with fairy lights to represent the stars of the lunar sky, to ensure heavenly blessings.

You Will Need

- branched willow or aspen bough
- silver spray paint
- pot or container
- river stones
- clear glass fairy lights (optional)
- silver totems
- white cotton thread
- thin blue ribbons
- silver crescents
- light blue, silver and/or white baubles
- seashells
- white or pastel paper or silk flowers
- 2 white candles
- matches

1 Spray your branch with silver paint and leave it to dry completely.

2 Stand the branch in a container and fill in around it with river stones to support it.

3 Decorate the moon tree with fairy lights, totems, ribbons, symbols and baubles, if you wish.

4 Empower your moon tree by lighting the fairy lights and two white nightlights at her base, repeating:
"Levanah, Queen of Heaven, I offer this sacred moon tree in your honour, and ask for your magical blessings to descend upon it."
Sit quietly and see what happens!

Index